1994

W9-CMP-121

AN INTRODUCTION TO MULTICULTURAL EDUCATION

James A. Banks
University of Washington, Seattle

Allyn and Bacon
Boston • London • Toronto • Sydney • Tokyo • Singapore

TO
Angela and Patricia, my children
To whom the torch will pass

Series Editor: Virginia Lanigan
Editorial Assistant: Nicole DePalma
Cover Administrator: Linda Dickinson
Manufacturing Buyer: Megan Cochran
Production Coordinator: Sheryl Avruch
Editorial-Production Service: TKM Productions

Copyright © 1994 by Allyn and Bacon
A Division of Simon & Schuster, Inc.
160 Gould Street
Needham Heights, Massachusetts 02194

Library of Congress Cataloging-in-Publication Data

Banks, James A.
   An introduction to multicultural education / James A. Banks.
     p. cm.
   Includes bibliographical references (p.   ) and index.
   ISBN 0-205-14910-3
   1. Multicultural education—United States. I. Title.
370.19'341—dc20   93–4782
                                                      CIP

Printed in the United States of America

10 9 8 7 6 5 4 3 2 1   98 97 96 95 94 93

CONTENTS

Preface   vi

1   Aims, Characteristics, Approaches   1

Aims of Multicultural Education   1
The Debate Over the Canon   2
Sharing Power   3
Facing Realities   3
Reinterpreting Western Civilization   4
Toward the Democratic Ideal   5
Educating for Freedom   7
Theoretical and Conceptual Work in Multicultural Education   7
Approaches to Multicultural Education   8
Characteristics of a Multicultural School   10
Ethnic Transformations and Changes: A Continuing Process   13

2   Curriculum Transformation   15

Confusion Over the Meaning of Multicultural Education   16
The Meaning and Goals of Multicultural Education   16
Multicultural Education Is for All Students   18
Challenges to the Mainstream Curriculum   19
Challenges to Multicultural Education   21
The Canon Battle: Special Interests Versus the Public Interest   22

School Knowledge and Multicultural Literacy   24
A Transformed Curriculum and Multiple Perspectives   24
Teaching Students to Know, to Care, and to Act   27
Multicultural Education and National Survival   29

3   School Reform and Intergroup Education   31

Demographic Trends and the Changing Workforce   31
America's Future   40
Intergroup Education   40
Guidelines for Reducing Prejudice in Students   44

4   Knowledge Components   47

The Four Knowledge Categories   47
Multicultural Education Paradigms   48
Concepts in Multicultural Education   50
Historical and Cultural Knowledge of Ethnic Groups   52

5   Teaching with Powerful Ideas   59

The Conceptual Approach   59
The Categories of Knowledge   60
A Conceptual Multicultural Curriculum   61
The Spiral Development of Concepts and Generalizations   62
Social Science and Value Inquiry Skills   64
Examples of Lessons Organized with Powerful Concepts   65
Teaching about Revolutions Using Social Science Inquiry   71
Value Inquiry in the Multicultural Curriculum   77
Conceptual Teaching and Curriculum Transformation   79

6   Education for Freedom
Ann Turnbaugh Lockwood Interviews James A. Banks   81

Multiple Voices, Multiple Perspectives   82
Two Old World Cultures Meet   83
Evidence to Support Multicultural Education   84
Changes for Teachers   86
Paradigm Shifts for Teachers   86
Contexts of Multicultural Education   87
One Nation United   89

7   Multicultural Benchmarks   91

A Policy Statement   91
The School Staff   93
Staff Attitudes and Expectations   94
The Curriculum   95
Teaching Strategies   96
Teaching Materials   96
Disproportionality   97
Parent Involvement   98
Monitoring   98

Glossary   101

Appendix A: The Academic Knowledge Components of
Multicultural Education: A Bibliography   105

Appendix B: Board of Education, City of New York
Statement of Policy on Multicultural Education and
Promotion of Positive Intergroup Relations,
November 9, 1989 (Amended)   109

Appendix C: A Multicultural Education
Evaluation Checklist   113

Appendix D: Ten Quick Ways to Analyze Children's
Books for Sexism and Racism   117

References   123

Index   132

PREFACE

Because of the enormous demographic changes in U.S. society, it is imperative for each classroom teacher and administrator to have a sophisticated understanding of the increasing racial, ethnic, cultural, and social-class diversity in the nation's schools and classrooms. To function effectively in multicultural classrooms and schools, educators need to acquire an understanding of the meaning of cultural and ethnic diversity in complex Western societies, to examine and clarify their racial and ethnic attitudes, and to develop the pedagogical knowledge and skills needed to work effectively with students from diverse cultural and ethnic groups.

This book is designed to introduce preservice and practicing educators to the major issues and concepts in multicultural education. It was written for readers who can devote only limited time to the topic. Chapter 1 discusses multicultural education goals, the canon debate, and approaches to multicultural education. It also identifies and describes the characteristics of a multicultural school. Chapter 2 describes the ways in which multicultural education seeks to transform the curriculum so that all students will acquire the knowledge, attitudes, and skills needed to become effective citizens in a pluralistic democratic society. The idea that multicultural education is in the nation's shared public interest is a key tenet of this chapter.

School reform and intergroup education are discussed in Chapter 3. The need to reform the nation's schools in order to respond to its demographic changes is examined in the first part of Chapter 3. The second part discusses intergroup education and the nature of students' racial attitudes. Guidelines for helping students to develop more positive racial attitudes and values are presented. School reform with goals related to both increasing academic achievement and helping students to develop more positive racial attitudes are essential if the United States is to compete effectively in an interdependent global society and help all students to become caring, committed, and active citizens.

The knowledge components that practicing educators need to acquire in order to function effectively in multicultural classrooms and schools are examined in Chapters 4 and 5. The types of knowledge needed by effective teachers are described in Chapter 4. This chapter also describes the major paradigms, key concepts, and powerful ideas, as well as the kinds of historical and cultural knowledge related to ethnic groups needed by today's educators. Chapter 6 discusses the characteristics of multicultural lessons and units that are organized around powerful ideas and concepts. It contains two teaching units that exemplify these characteristics.

Chapters 6 and 7 highlight and summarize some of the major issues, concepts, and discourses in multicultural education. In the interview that constitutes Chapter 6, I revisit and further clarify some of the issues discussed in earlier chapters. I summarize the book in Chapter 7 with a discussion of major benchmarks that can be used to determine whether a school or educational institution is actualizing multicultural education in its best and deepest sense.

This book was written to provide readers with a brief, comprehensive overview of multicultural education, a grasp of its complexity, and a helpful understanding of what it means for educational practice. Readers who wish to study multicultural education in greater depth will find the references at the end of the book a helpful resource. I hope this book will start readers on an enriching path in multicultural education that will continue and deepen throughout their careers.

ACKNOWLEDGMENTS

I would like to thank Cherry A. McGee Banks for being a colleague and friend who always listens and responds with thoughtful and keen insights. I would also like to thank her for reading an earlier draft of this book and making helpful suggestions and for preparing the index. I am grateful to five other individuals who read the book in manuscript form and made thoughtful comments that enabled me to strengthen it: Harold Chu, George Mason University; Carlos F. Diaz, Florida Atlantic University; Ricardo L. Garcia, the University of Idaho; Judith Green, Kansas State University; and Tonya Huber, Wichita State University. The comments of my colleagues were helpful. However, I am totally responsible for the contents of this book.

I would like to thank my colleagues in the College of Education and the Center for Multicultural Education—especially Geneva Gay, Nancy Hansen-Krening, Michael S. Knapp, and Walter C. Parker— for stimulating conversations about race, class, diversity, and education. These colleagues help to make the College and the Center rich intellectual communities.

In writing this book, I drew freely from some of some of my recent articles and other publications. I wish to thank the following organizations and publishers for giving me permission to use the works that I authored:

The Association for Supervision and Curriculum Development for "Multicultural Education: For Freedom's Sake," *Educational Leadership, 49* (December, 1991/January, 1992), pp. 32–36.

The National Education Association for "Multicultural Education: Nature, Challenges, and Opportunities," in Carlos F. Diaz (Ed.) *Multicultural Education for the 21st Century* (pp. 23–37). Washington, DC, 1992; and "Multiethnic Education and School Reform," in Lois V. Edinger, Paul L. Houts, & Dorothy V. Meyer (Eds.) *Education in the 80s: Curricular Challenges* (pp. 112–123). Washington, DC, 1981.

The Southwest Educational Development Laboratory for *Preparing Teachers and Administrators in a Multicultural Society.* Austin, TX, 1990.

Pi Lambda Theta for "Multicultural Literacy and Curriculum Reform," *Educational Horizons, 69* (Spring 1991), pp. 135–140.

The National Council for the Social Studies for "Reducing Prejudice in Children: Guidelines from Research," *Social Studies and the Young Learner, 5* (November/December, 1992), pp. 3–5.

The Educational Materials and Service Center for "Approaches to Multicultural Curriculum Reform, " *Multicultural Leader, 1* (Spring, 1988), pp. 1–3.

Longman for Figure 3.1 and Table 15.3 from James A. Banks, with Ambrose A. Clegg, Jr., *Teaching Strategies for the Social Studies: Inquiry, Valuing and Decision-Making,* 4th edition (pp. 79 and 445). New York, 1990.

The National Center for Effective Schools Research and Development (Madison, WI) for Anne Turnbaugh Lockwood, "Education for Freedom" (interview with James A. Banks), *Focus in Change, 1* (Summer, 1992), pp. 3–7.

The lesson in Chapter 5 on "Columbus and the Arawaks" is adapted from James A. Banks, with Sam L. Sebesta, *We Americans: Our History and People* (Vol. 1). Boston: Allyn and Bacon, 1982, pp. 35–43. The rights to this book are owned by the authors. I wish to thank Sam L. Sebesta for his permission to use the lesson in this book.

James A. Banks
Seattle, Washington

1

AIMS, CHARACTERISTICS, AND APPROACHES

In *The Dialectic of Freedom,* Maxine Greene (1988) asks, "What does it mean to be a citizen of the free world?" It means, she concluded, having the capacity to choose, the power to act to attain one's purposes, and the ability to help transform a world lived in common with others. An important factor that limits human freedom in a pluralistic society is the cultural encapsulation into which all individuals are socialized. People learn the values, beliefs, and stereotypes of their community cultures. Although these community cultures enable individuals to survive, they also restrict their freedom and ability to make critical choices and to take actions to help reform society.

AIMS OF MULTICULTURAL EDUCATION

Education within a pluralistic society should affirm and help students understand their home and community cultures. However, it should also help free them from their cultural boundaries. To create and maintain a civic community that works for the common good, education in a democratic society should help students acquire the knowledge, attitudes, and skills they will need to participate in civic action to make society more equitable and just.

Multicultural education is an education for freedom (Parekh, 1986) that is essential in today's ethnically polarized and troubled world. It has evoked a divisive national debate, in part because of the divergent views that citizens hold about what constitutes an American identity and

1

about the roots and nature of American civilization. In turn, the debate has sparked a power struggle over who should participate in formulating the canon used to shape the curriculum in the nation's schools, colleges, and universities.

THE DEBATE OVER THE CANON

A chorus of strident voices has launched an orchestrated and widely publicized attack on the movement to infuse content about ethnic groups and women into the school and university curriculum. Much of the current debate over multicultural education has taken place in mass media publications such as *Time* (Gray, 1991), the *Wall Street Journal* (Sirkin, 1990), and the *New Republic* (Howe, 1991), rather than in scholarly journals and forums. The Western traditionalists (writers who defend the canon now within the schools and universities) and the multiculturalists rarely engage in reflective dialogue. Rather, scholars on each side of the debate marshal data to support their briefs and ignore facts, interpretations, and perspectives that are inconsistent with their positions and visions of the present and future.

In his book, *Illiberal Education,* D'Souza (1991) defends the existing curriculum and structures in higher education while presenting an alarming picture of where multiculturalism is taking the nation. Schlesinger (1991) argues that the multicultural movement is disuniting America. Few of the critics, including Schlesinger, bother to distinguish Afrocentrism from multicultural education. When multiculturalists respond to such criticism, they often fail to describe the important ways in which the multicultural vision is consistent with the democratic ideals of the West and with the heritage of Western civilization. The multicultural literature pays too little attention to the fact that the multicultural education movement emerged out of Western democratic ideals. One of its major aims is to close the gap between the Western democratic ideals of equality and justice and societal practices that contradict those ideals, such as discrimination based on race, gender, and social class.

Because so much of the debate over the canon has taken place in the popular media, which encourages simplistic, sound-byte explanations, the issues related to the curriculum canon have been overdrawn and oversimplified by advocates on both sides. The result is that the debate often generates more heat than light. Various interest groups have been polarized rather than encouraged to exchange ideas that might help us find creative solutions to the problems related to race, ethnicity, gender, and schooling.

As the ethnic texture of the nation deepens, problems related to diversity will intensify rather than diminish. Consequently, we need leaders and educators of goodwill, from all political and ideological persuasions, to participate in genuine discussions, dialogues, and debates that will help us formulate visionary and workable solutions and enable us to deal creatively with the challenges posed by the increasing diversity in the United States and the world. We must learn how to transform the problems related to racial and ethnic diversity into opportunities and strengths.

SHARING POWER

Western traditionalists and multiculturalists must realize that they are entering into the debate from different power positions. Western traditionalists hold the balance of power, financial resources, and the top positions in the mass media, schools, colleges and universities, government, and the publishing industry. Genuine discussion between the traditionalists and the multiculturalists can take place only when power is placed on the table, negotiated, and shared.

Despite all of the rhetoric about the extent to which Chaucer, Shakespeare, Milton, and other Western writers are threatened by the onslaught of women and writers of color into the curriculum, the reality is that the curriculum in the nation's schools and universities is largely Western in its concepts, paradigms, and content. Applebee (1989) finds that traditional Western writers, such as Shakespeare and Milton, dominate the required reading lists in high school English courses. Graff (1992) finds that traditional Western writers also dominate the required reading lists in a college curriculum that he analyzed.

Concepts such as the Middle Ages and the Renaissance are still used to organize most units in history, literature, and the arts. When content about African and Asian cultures is incorporated into the curriculum, it is usually viewed within the context of European concepts and paradigms. For example, Asian, African, and American histories are often studied under the topic, "The Age of Discovery," which means the time when Europeans first arrived in these lands. The Americas are often referred to as the New World.

FACING REALITIES

If they are to achieve a productive dialogue rather than a polarizing debate, both the Western traditionalists and the multiculturalists must face some facts. The growing number of people of color in our society and schools constitutes a demographic imperative educators must hear and respond to. The 1990 census indicated that one of every four Americans is a person of color. By the turn of the century, one of every three will be of color (Commission on Minority Participation, 1988). Nearly half of the nation's students will be of color by 2020 (Pallas, Natriello, & McDill, 1989). Although the school and university curriculums remain Western oriented, this growing number of people of color will increasingly demand to share power in curriculum decision-making and in shaping a curriculum canon that reflects their experiences, histories, struggles, and victories.

People of color, women, and other marginalized groups are demanding that their voices, visions, and perspectives be included in the curriculum. They ask that the debt Western civilization owes to Africa, Asia, and indigenous America be acknowledged (Allen, 1986; Bernal, 1987). Advocates of the Afrocentric curriculum, in sometimes passionate language that reflects a dream long deferred, are merely asking that the cultures of Africa and African American people be legitimized in the curriculum and that the African contributions to European civilization be acknowledged. People of color and women are also demanding that the facts about their victimization be told, not only for truth's sake but also because they need to better understand their conditions so that they and others can work to reform society.

However, these groups must acknowledge that they do not want to eliminate Aristotle, Shakespeare, or Western civilization from the school curriculum. To reject the West would be to reject important aspects of their own cultural heritages, experiences, and identities. The most important scholarly and literary works written by African Americans, such as works by W. E. B. DuBois (1935), Carter G. Woodson (1921), and Zora Neale Hurston (1978), are expressions of Western cultural experiences. African American culture resulted from a blending of diverse African cultural characteristics with those of Native American and European ethnic groups in the United States.

REINTERPRETING WESTERN CIVILIZATION

Rather than excluding Western civilization from the curriculum, multiculturalists want a more truthful, complex, and diverse version of the West taught in the schools. They want the curriculum to describe the ways in which African, Asian, and indigenous American cultures have influenced and interacted with Western civilization. They also want schools to discuss not only the diversity and democratic ideals of Western civilization, but also its failures, tensions, and dilemmas, and the struggles by various groups in Western societies to realize their dreams against great odds.

We need to deconstruct the myth that the West is homogeneous, that it owes few debts to other world civilizations, and that only privileged and upper-status Europeans and European American males have been its key actors. Weatherford (1992) describes the debt the West owes to the first Americans. Bernal (1987), Drake (1987), Van Sertima (1984), and Clarke (1990) marshal considerable amounts of historical and cultural data that describe the ways in which African and Afroasiatic cultures influenced the development of Western civilization. Bernal, for example, presents linguistic and archaeological evidence to substantiate his claim that important parts of Greek civilization (technologies, language, deities, and architecture) originated in ancient Africa.

We should teach students that knowledge is a social construction, that it reflects the perspectives, experiences, and values of the people and cultures that construct it, and that it is dynamic, changing, and debated among knowledge creators and users (Banks, 1991a). Rather than keep such knowledge debates as the extent to which African civilizations contributed to Western civilization out of the classroom, teachers should make them an integral part of teaching. The classroom should become a forum in which multicultural debates concerning the construction of knowledge take place (Banks, 1993a). The voices of Western traditionalists, multiculturalists, textbook authors, and radical writers should be heard and legitimized in the classroom.

TOWARD THE DEMOCRATIC IDEAL

The fact that multiculturalists want to reformulate and transform the Western canon—not to purge the curriculum of the West—is absent from most of the writings of the Western traditionalists. It doesn't support their argument that Shakespeare, Milton, and Aristotle are endangered. By the same token, the multiculturalists have written little about the intersections of multicultural content and a Westerncentric canon, perhaps because they have focused on ways in which the established Western canon should be reconstructed and transformed.

Multicultural education itself is a product of the West. It grew out of a struggle guided by Western ideals for human dignity, equality, and freedom (Parker, 1991). Multicultural education is a child of the Civil Rights Movement led by African Americans that was designed to eliminate discrimination in housing, public accommodation, and other areas. The leaders of the Civil Rights Movement, such as Fannie Lou Hamer,

Rosa Parks (Parks with Haskins, 1992), and Daisy Bates (1987), internalized the American democratic ideal stated in such important United States documents as the Declaration of Independence, the Constitution, and the Bill of Rights. The civil rights leaders of the 1960s and 1970s used the Western ideals of freedom and democracy to justify and legitimize their push for structural inclusion and the end of institutionalized discrimination and racism.

The Civil Rights Movement of the 1960s echoed throughout the United States and the world. Other groups, such as Native Americans and Hispanics, women, and people with disabilities, initiated their own freedom movements. These cultural revitalization movements made demands on a number of institutions. The nation's schools and universities became primary targets for reform, in part because they were important symbols of the structural exclusion that marginalized groups experienced and in part because they were easily accessible.

It would be a serious mistake to interpret these cultural revitalization movements and the educational reforms they gave birth to as a repudiation of the West and Western civilization. The major goals of these movements are full inclusion of the marginalized groups into Western institutions and a reform of these institutions so that their practices are more consistent with their democratic ideals. Multicultural education not only arose out of Western traditions and ideals, its major goal is to create a nation-state that actualizes the democratic ideals for all that the Founding Fathers intended for an elite few. Rather than being divisive, as some critics contend, multicultural education is designed to reduce race, class, and gender divisions in the United States and the world.

Given the tremendous social-class and racial cleavages in U.S. society, it is inaccurate to claim that the study of ethnic diversity will threaten national cohesion. The real threats to national unity—which in an economic, sociological, and psychological sense we have not fully attained but are working toward—are the deepening racial and social-class schisms within U.S. society. As Wilson (1987) points out in *The Truly Disadvantaged,* the gap between the rich and the poor grew tremendously during the 1980s. The social-class schism has occurred not only across racial and ethnic groups but within these groups. Hence, the rush to the suburbs has not just been a White flight but has been a flight by the middle class of many hues. As a consequence, low-income African Americans, Asian Americans, and Hispanics have been left in inner-city communities without the middle-class members of their groups to provide needed leadership and role models. They are more excluded than ever from mainstream U.S. society.

EDUCATING FOR FREEDOM

Each of us becomes culturally encapsulated during our socialization in childhood. We accept the assumptions of our own community culture and internalize its values, views of the universe, misconceptions, and stereotypes. Although this is as true for the child socialized within a mainstream culture as it is for the minority child, minority children are usually forced to examine, confront, and question their cultural assumptions when they enter school.

Students who are born and socialized within the mainstream culture of a society rarely have an opportunity to identify, question, and challenge their cultural assumptions, beliefs, values, and perspectives because the school culture usually reinforces those that they learn at home and in their communities. Consequently, mainstream Americans have few opportunities to become free of cultural assumptions and perspectives that are monocultural, that devalue African and Asian cultures, and that stereotype people of color and people who are poor, or who are victimized in other ways. These mainstream Americans often have an inability to function effectively within other American cultures, as well as an inability to experience and benefit from cross-cultural participation and relationships.

To participate fully in our democratic society, these students and all students need the skills a multicultural education can give them to understand others and to thrive in a rapidly changing, diverse world. Thus, the debate between the Western traditionalists and the multiculturalists fits well within the tradition of a pluralistic democratic society. Its final result will most likely be not exactly what either side wants, but a synthesized and compromised perspective that will provide a new vision for the nation as we enter the twenty-first century.

THEORETICAL AND CONCEPTUAL WORK IN MULTICULTURAL EDUCATION

Despite the bitter and divisive debates that it has evoked, major theoretical and conceptual work has been done in multicultural education within the last 20 years (Banks, 1973, 1988a; Banks & Lynch, 1986; Lynch, 1986; Modgil, Verma, Mallick, & Modgil, 1986; Sleeter & Grant, 1988, Verma, 1989). The doomsayers predicted that multicultural education was merely another passing fad. However, there is increasing evidence that it is becoming institutionalized within U.S. schools, colleges, and universities. The increasing acceptance of multicultural education in U.S. education is related to a number of educational, sociological, and demographic developments that are described in Chapter 3.

APPROACHES TO MULTICULTURAL EDUCATION

There are many different strategies, definitions, and approaches to multicultural education in the United States (Banks & Banks, 1993; Sleeter & Grant, 1987). However, at least three major groups of approaches can be identified: curriculum reform, achievement, and intergroup education (see Table 1–1). This typology is an ideal type of conceptualization; it approximates but does not describe reality in its total complexity. There are many different conceptions, strategies, and paradigms within each of these three major approaches. Also, the approaches are not mutually exclusive.

Curriculum reform approaches conceptualize multicultural education as a process that involves additions to or changes in the content of the school or university curriculum. The primary goal of these approaches is to incorporate the voices, experiences, and struggles of ethnic, cultural, and gender groups into the curriculum. The various approaches within this category vary greatly in conceptions, goals, and results. Four approaches to multicultural curriculum reform that I conceptualized are discussed in Chapter 2: (1) contributions, (2) additive, (3) transformation, and (4) decision-making and social action.

Achievement approaches conceptualize multicultural education as a set of goals, theories, and strategies designed to increase the academic achievement of low-income students, students of color, women, and students with disabilities. Achievement issues are discussed in Chapter 3. Two major conceptions within these approaches are the cultural deprivation and the cultural difference paradigms (Banks, 1988b). These paradigms are examined in Chapter 4. The *cultural deprivation* paradigm dominated the discussion of the education of people of color and lower-class students in the 1960s but was seriously challenged by the *cultural difference* paradigm during the 1970s and early 1980s. However, the cultural deprivation paradigm is gaining renewed popularity in the United States. Low-income students are often referred to as *students-at-risk* (Cuban, 1989; Richardson, Casanova, Placier, & Guilfoyle, 1989).

The primary goal of *intergroup education approaches* is to help students develop more positive attitudes toward people from different racial, cultural, and gender groups. Another important goal is to help members of marginalized groups—such as racial groups, women, and people with disabilities—to develop more positive feelings toward

TABLE 1–1   Approaches to Multicultural Education

Approach	Description	Major Goals	Examples of Practices
Curriculum Reform	A process that involves additions to or changes in the content of the curriculum	To incorporate content about cultural groups into the curriculum To enable students to look at a curriculum content from new and different perspectives To transform the canon and paradigms on which the curriculum is based	Celebration of cultural heroes and holidays Multicultural curriculum guides Multicultural content workshops for teachers and administrators Textbooks that incorporate multicultural content
Achievement	A set of theories, practices, and strategies designed to increase the academic achievement of lower-class students, students of color, women, and students with disabilities	To increase the academic achievement of students from different ethnic, cultural, and gender groups	Programs that match teaching styles with the learning styles of students Bilingual-bicultural education programs Language programs that incorporate the language and culture of African American students Special math and science programs for female students
Intergroup Education	Knowledge, content, and processes designed to help students develop democratic intergroup attitudes and values	To help students develop positive attitudes toward diverse racial, ethnic, and cultural groups To help members of victimized and marginalized groups develop more positive attitudes toward their own cultural group	Prejudice-reduction projects, such as the World of Difference Project, sponsored by the Anti-Defamation League of B'nai B'rith Desegregated schools, classrooms, and programs Cooperative learning strategies and techniques

their own groups. Intergroup education approaches are discussed in Chapter 3.

Although it is a slow and sometimes painful process, elements of each of these major approaches to multicultural education are becoming institutionalized within the schools, colleges, and universities in the United States and in other Western nations such as Australia, Canada, and the United Kingdom (Banks & Lynch, 1986; Verma, 1989).

CHARACTERISTICS OF A MULTICULTURAL SCHOOL

Multicultural education is an educational reform movement designed to restructure schools and other educational institutions so that students from all social-class, racial, cultural, and gender groups will have an equal opportunity to learn (Banks & Banks, 1993). Another important goal of multicultural education is to help all students develop more democratic values and beliefs and the knowledge, skills, and attitudes needed to function cross-culturally.

What parts of the school are targets of multicultural educational reform? A multicultural school has the eight characteristics listed in Table 1–2. Consequently, school reform is targeted on the following school variables:

1. *Attitudes, perceptions, beliefs, and actions of the school staff.* Research indicates that teachers and administrators often have low expectations for language minority students (Cortés, 1986; Heath, 1983; Ovando & Collier, 1985), low-income students, and students of color (Percell, 1993; Philips, 1983). In a restructured multicultural school, teachers and administrators have high academic expectations for all students and believe that all students can learn (Brookover et al., 1979; Edmonds, 1986).

2. *Formalized curriculum and course of study.* The curriculum in most schools, which is Anglocentric and Eurocentric, shows most concepts, events, and situations from the perspectives of mainstream Americans (Applebee, 1989). It often marginalizes the experiences of people of color and women. Multicultural education reforms the curriculum so that students view events, concepts, issues, and problems from the perspectives of diverse racial, ethnic, and social-class groups (Banks, 1991a). The perspectives of both men and women are also important in the restructured, multicultural curriculum.

TABLE 1–2 The Eight Characteristics of the Multicultural School

1. The teachers and school administrators have expectations for all students and positive attitudes toward them. They also respond to them in positive and caring ways.
2. The formalized curriculum reflects the experiences, cultures, and perspectives of a range of cultural and ethnic groups as well as both genders.
3. The teaching styles used by the teachers match the learning, cultural, and motivational styles of the students.
4. The teachers and administrators show respect for the students' first languages and dialects.
5. The instructional materials used in the school show events, situations, and concepts from the perspectives of a range of cultural, ethnic, and racial groups.
6. The assessment and testing procedures used in the school are culturally sensitive and result in students of color being represented proportionately in classes for the gifted and talented.
7. The school culture and the hidden curriculum reflect cultural and ethnic diversity.
8. The school counselors have high expectations for students from different racial, ethnic, and language groups and help these students to set and realize positive career goals.

3. *Learning, teaching, and cultural styles favored by the school.* Research indicates that a large number of low-income, linguistic minority, Hispanic, Native American, and African American students have learning, cultural, and motivational styles that differ from the teaching styles that are used most frequently in the schools (Delpit, 1988; Ramírez & Castañeda, 1974; Shade, 1989). These students often learn best when cooperative rather than competitive teaching techniques are used (Slavin, 1983; Cohen, 1986; Stahl & VanSickle, 1992). Many of them also learn best when school rules and learning outcomes are made explicit and expectations are made clear (Delpit, 1988).

4. *Languages and dialects of the school.* Many students come to school speaking languages and dialects of English that differ from the standard English taught in the school. Although all students must learn standard English in order to function successfully in the wider society, the school should respect the first languages and dialects of students. Many African American students come to school speaking what many linguistics call *Ebonics* or "Black English" (Smitherman, 1977). In the restructured, multicultural school, teachers and administrators respect the languages and dialects of English that stu-

dents come to school speaking and use the students' first languages and dialects as vehicles for helping them to learn standard English (Heath, 1983; Ovando & Collier, 1985).

5. *Instructional materials.* Many biases, sometimes latent, are found in textbooks and other instructional materials (Apple & Christian-Smith, 1991). These materials often marginalize the experiences of people of color, women, and low-income people and focus on the perspectives of men who are members of the mainstream society. In the restructured, multicultural school, instructional materials are reformed and depict events from diverse ethnic and cultural perspectives. Teachers and students are also taught to identify and challenge the biases and assumptions of all materials.

6. *Assessment and testing procedures.* IQ and other mental-ability tests often result in students of color, low-income students, and linguistic minority students being overrepresented in classes for mentally retarded students and underrepresented in classes for gifted and talented students (Patton, 1992). Human talent, as well as mental retardation, is randomly distributed across human populations (Gardner, 1983). Consequently, in a restructured multicultural school, assessment techniques are used that enable students from diverse cultural and ethnic groups to be assessed in culturally fair and just ways (Mercer, 1989; Samuda, 1975). In a restructured, multicultural school, students of color and language minority students are found proportionately in classes for the gifted and talented. They are not heavily concentrated in classes for mentally retarded students.

7. *The school culture and the hidden curriculum.* The *hidden curriculum* has been defined as the curriculum that no teacher explicitly teaches but that all students learn. The school's attitudes toward cultural and ethnic diversity is reflected in many subtle ways in the school culture, such as the kinds of pictures on the bulletin boards, the racial composition of the school staff, and the fairness with which students from different racial, cultural, and ethnic groups are disciplined and suspended. Multicultural education reforms the total school environment so that the hidden curriculum sends the message that cultural and ethnic diversity is valued and celebrated.

8. *The counseling program.* In an effective multicultural school, counselors help students from diverse cultural, racial, and ethnic groups to make effective career choices and to take the courses needed to pursue those career choices (Sue, 1981). Multiculturally oriented counselors also help students to reach beyond their grasp, to dream, and to actualize their dreams.

Multicultural educators make the assumption that if the preceding eight variables within the school environment are reformed and restructured, students from diverse ethnic, cultural, language, and gender groups will attain higher levels of academic achievement and the intergroup attitudes and beliefs of students from all groups will become more democratic.

ETHNIC TRANSFORMATIONS AND CHANGES: A CONTINUING PROCESS

As the ethnic texture of nations such as the United States and Canada continues to deepen, educational programs related to ethnic and cultural diversity will continue to emerge and take various shapes and forms. New challenges will continue to evolve in pluralistic democratic societies. The extent to which these challenges will be transformed into opportunities will be largely dependent on the vision, knowledge, and commitment of the nation's educators. You will have to take a stand on multicultural education and determine what actions related to it you will take in your classroom and school. The chapters in this book are designed to help you conceptualize and take informed and reflective actions that will make your school a more caring and humane place for students.

2

CURRICULUM
TRANSFORMATION

It is important to distinguish curriculum *infusion* and curriculum *transformation*. When the curriculum is infused with ethnic and gender content without curriculum transformation, the students view the experiences of ethnic groups and women from the perspectives and conceptual frameworks of the traditional Western canon. Consequently, groups such as Native Americans, Asian Americans, and Hispanics are added to the curriculum but their experiences are viewed from the perspective of mainstream historians and social scientists. When curriculum infusion occurs without transformation, women are added to the curriculum but are viewed from the perspectives of mainstream males. Concepts such as "The Westward Movement," "The European Discovery of America," and "Men and Their Families Went West" remain intact.

When curriculum transformation occurs, students and teachers make paradigm shifts and view the American and world experience from the perspectives of different racial, ethnic, cultural, and gender groups. Columbus's arrival in the Americas is no longer viewed as a "discovery" but as a cultural *contact* or *encounter* (Golden et al, 1991; Rouse, 1992; Stannard, 1992) that had very different consequences for the Tainos (Arawaks), Europeans, and Africans. In a transformed curriculum, the experiences of women in the West are not viewed as an appendage to the experience of men but are viewed "through women's eyes" (Armitage, 1987).

This chapter discusses the confusion over goals in multicultural education, describes its goals and challenges, and states the rationale for a transformative multicultural curriculum. An important goal of multicultural education is to help teachers and students transform their thinking about the nature and development of the United States and the world and to develop a commitment to act in ways that will make the United States a more democratic and just nation.

CONFUSION OVER THE MEANING OF MULTICULTURAL EDUCATION

A great deal of confusion exists, among both educators and the general public, about the meaning of multicultural education. The meaning of multicultural education among these groups varies from education about people in other lands to educating African American students about their heritage but teaching them little about the Western heritage of the United States. The confusion over the meaning of multicultural education was indicated by a question the editor of a national education publication asked me: "What is the difference between multicultural education, ethnocentric education, and global education?" Later during the telephone interview, I discovered that she had meant "Afrocentric education" rather than "ethnocentric education." To her, these terms were synonymous.

THE MEANING AND GOALS OF MULTICULTURAL EDUCATION

Before we can solve the problem caused by the multiple meanings of multicultural education, we need to better understand its causes. One important cause of the confusion over the meaning of multicultural education is the multiple meanings of the concept in the professional literature itself. Sleeter and Grant (1987), in their comprehensive survey of the literature on multicultural education, found that the term has diverse meanings and that about the only commonality that the various definitions share is reform designed to improve schooling for students of color.

To advance the field and to reduce the multiple meanings of multicultural education, scholars need to develop a higher level of consensus about what the concept means. Agreement about the meaning of multicultural education is emerging among academics. A consensus is developing among scholars that an important goal of multicultural education is to increase educational equality for both gender groups, for students from diverse ethnic and cultural groups, and for exceptional students (Banks & Banks, 1993; Sleeter & Grant, 1988). A major assumption of multicultural education is that some groups of students—because their cultural characteristics are more consistent with the culture, norms, and expectations of the school than other groups of students—

have greater opportunities for academic success than students whose cultures are less consistent with the school culture. Low-income African American males, for example, tend to have more problems in schools than middle-class Anglo males (Gibbs, 1988).

Because one of its goals is to increase educational equality for students from diverse groups, school restructuring is essential to make multicultural education become a reality. To restructure schools in order to provide all students with an equal chance to learn, some of the major assumptions, beliefs, and structures within schools must be radically changed. These include tracking and the ways in which mental ability tests are interpreted and used (Oakes, 1992; Mercer, 1989). New paradigms about the ways students learn, about human ability (Gardner, 1983; Gould, 1981), and about the nature of knowledge will have to be institutionalized in order to restructure schools and make multicultural education a reality. Teachers will have to believe that all students can learn, regardless of their social-class or ethnic-group membership, and that knowledge is a social construction that has social, political, and normative assumptions (Code, 1991; Harding, 1991; Collins, 1990). Implementing multicultural education within a school is a continuous process that cannot be implemented within a few weeks or over several years. The implementation of multicultural education requires a long-term commitment to school improvement and restructuring.

Another important goal of multicultural education—on which there is wide consensus among authorities in the field but which is neither understood nor appreciated by many teachers, journalists, and the public—is to help all students, including White mainstream students, to develop the knowledge, skills, and attitudes they will need to survive and function effectively in a future U.S. society in which one out of every three people will be a person of color. Our survival as a strong and democratic nation will be seriously imperiled if we do not help our students attain the knowledge and skills they need to function in a culturally diverse future society and world. As Martin Luther King stated eloquently, "We will live together as brothers and sisters or die separate and apart as strangers" (King, 1987).

This goal of multicultural education is related to an important goal of global education. An important aim of global education is to help students to develop cross-cultural competency in cultures beyond our national boundaries and the insights and understandings needed to understand how all peoples living on the earth have highly interconnected fates (Becker, 1979). Citizens who have an understanding and empathy for the cultures within their own nation are probably more likely to function effectively in cultures outside of their nation than citizens who have little understanding and empathy for cultures within their own society.

Although multicultural and global education share some important aims, in practice global education can hinder teaching about ethnic and cultural diversity in the United States. Some teachers are more comfortable teaching about Mexico than they are teaching about Mexican Americans who live within their own cities and states. Other teachers, as well as some publishers, do not distinguish *multicultural* and *global* education. Although the goals of multicultural and global education are complimentary, they need to be distinguished both conceptually and in practice.

MULTICULTURAL EDUCATION IS FOR ALL STUDENTS

We need to think seriously about why multicultural educators have not been more successful in conveying to teachers, journalists, and the general public the idea that multicultural education is concerned not only with ethnic minority and linguistically diverse students but with White mainstream students. It is also not widely acknowledged that many of the reforms designed to increase the academic achievement of ethnic and linguistic minority students, such as a pedagogy that is sensitive to student learning styles and cooperative learning techniques, will also help White mainstream students to increase their academic achievement and to develop more positive intergroup attitudes and values (Slavin, 1983; Shade, 1989).

It is important for multicultural education to be conceptualized as a strategy for all students for several important reasons. U.S. schools are not working as well as they should be to prepare all students to function in a highly technological, postindustrial society (Bell, 1973; Graham, 1992). Most students of color (with the important exception of some groups of Asian students such as Chinese and Japanese Americans) and low-income students are more dependent on the school for academic achievement than are White middle-class students for a variety of complex reasons. However, school restructuring is needed for all students because of the high level of literacy and skills needed by citizens in a knowledge society and because of the high expectations that the public has for today's schools. Public expectations for the common schools have increased tremendously since the turn of the century when many school leavers were able to get jobs in factories (Cremin, 1989; Graham, 1992). School restructuring is an important and major aim of multicultural education.

Multicultural education should also be conceptualized as a strategy for all students because it will become institutionalized and supported in the nation's schools, colleges, and universities only to the extent that it is perceived as universal and in the broad public interest. An ethnic-specific notion of multicultural education stands little chance of success and implementation in the nation's educational institutions.

CHALLENGES TO THE
MAINSTREAM CURRICULUM

Some readers might rightly claim that an ethnic-specific curriculum and education already exists in the nation's educational institutions and that it is Eurocentric and male dominated. I would agree with this claim but believe that the days for the primacy and dominance of the mainstream curriculum are limited. The curriculum that is institutionalized within our nation's schools, colleges, and universities is being seriously challenged today and will continue to be challenged until it is revised to more accurately reflect the experiences, voices, and struggles of people of color, women, and other cultural and social-class groups in U.S. society.

My claim that only an inclusive multicultural education can become institutionalized needs further discussion because an Anglocentric, male-oriented curriculum dominates the schools and university curriculum today (Applebee, 1989; Graff, 1992). Applebee (1992) found that of the 10 most frequently assigned required book-length works taught in the high school grades, only 1 title was by a female author (Harper Lee, *To Kill A Mockingbird*) and none were by a writer of color. Works by Shakespeare, Steinbeck, and Dickens led the list.

However, multicultural works have made important inroads into the mainstream curriculum within the last 20 years. Important inroads will increasingly be made in the future. In the elementary and high school grades, much more ethnic content appears in social studies and language arts textbooks today than was the case in the 1960s (Garcia, in press). Also, some teachers assign works written by authors of color along with more standard American classics. In his study of book-length works used in the high schools, Applebee (1992) concludes that his most striking finding was how similar present reading lists are to past ones and how little change has occurred. However, he notes that many teachers use anthologies as a mainstay of their literature programs and that 21 percent of the anthology selections were written by women and 14 percent by authors of color.

The dominance of the mainstream curriculum is much less complete and tenacious than it was before the Civil Rights and Women's Rights Movements of the 1960s and 1970s. The historical, social, and economic

factors are different today than they were when Anglo Americans established control over the nation's major social, economic, and political
institutions in the seventeenth and eighteenth centuries. The economic,
demographic, and ideological factors that led to the establishment of
Anglo hegemony early in our nation's history are changing, even
though Anglo Americans are still politically, economically, and culturally dominant, as Supreme Court decisions that slowed the pace of
affirmative action initiatives during the 1980s indicated.

Nevertheless, there are signs throughout U.S. society that Anglo
dominance and hegemony is being challenged and that groups such as
African Americans, Asian Americans, and Hispanics are increasingly
demanding full structural inclusion and a reformulation of the canon
used to select content for the school, college, and university curriculum
(Butler & Walter, 1991; Graff, 1992). It is also important to realize that
many compassionate and informed Whites are joining people of color
to support reforms in the nation's social, economic, political, and educational institutions. It would be a mistake to conceptualize or perceive
the reform movements today as people of color versus Whites.

One of the pervasive myths within our society is that Whites are a
monolithic group. The word *White* conceals more than it reveals. Whites
are a very diverse group in terms of ethnic and cultural characteristics,
political affiliations, and attitudes toward ethnic and cultural diversity.
Many Whites today, as well as historically, have supported social movements to increase the rights of African Americans and other people of
color (Branch, 1988). Reform-oriented White citizens who are pushing
for a more equitable and just society are an important factor that will
make it increasingly difficult for the Anglo-Saxon vision to continue to
dominate our educational institutions.

Whites today are playing an important role in social reform movements and in the election of African American and Hispanic politicians.
Many White students on university campuses are forming coalitions
with students of color to demand that the university curriculum be
reformed to include content about people of color and women. The
student movements that are demanding ethnic studies requirements on
university campuses have experienced major victories. The list of universities that have implemented ethnic studies requirements grows
longer each year. It includes the University of Minnesota-Twin Cities,
the University of California-Berkeley, and the University of Michigan,
Ann Arbor.

The Anglocentric curriculum will continue to be challenged until it
is reformed to include the voices and experiences of a range of ethnic
and cultural groups. The significant percentage of people of color, including African Americans and Hispanics, who are in positions of leadership in educational institutions will continue to work to get the

experiences of their people integrated into the school and university curriculum. These individuals include researchers, professors, administrators, and authors of textbooks. Students of color will continue to form coalitions with reform-oriented White students and demand that the school and university curriculum be reformed to reflect the ethnic and cultural reality of American life. Demographers project that students of color will make up about 46 percent of the nation's school-age youths (ages 0 to 17) by 2020 (Pallas, Natriello, & McDill, 1989). Parents and community groups will continue to demand that the school and university curriculum be reformed to give voice to their experiences and struggles. African American parents and community groups are the major agents pushing for a curriculum that reflects African civilizations and experimental schools for Black males (Chmelynski, 1990; Lee, 1992).

Feminists will continue to challenge the mainstream curriculum because many of them view it as male-centric, patriarchal, and sexist. Much of the new research in women studies deals with the cultures of women of color (Anderson & Collins, 1992; Jones, 1985). Women studies and ethnic studies will continue to interconnect and challenge the dominant curriculum in the nation's schools, colleges, and universities.

CHALLENGES TO MULTICULTURAL EDUCATION

I have argued that an ethnic-specific version of multicultural education is not likely to become institutionalized within the nation's schools, colleges, and universities and that the days of Anglo hegemony in the U.S. curriculum are limited. This is admittedly a long-view of our society and future. Multicultural education is now facing a strenuous and well-orchestrated challenge from conservative groups and scholars (D'Souza, 1991; Schlesinger, 1991). This challenge will continue, will be fierce, and will at times become ugly and pernicious. It will take diverse forms, expressions, and shapes. I believe that part of the confused meanings of multicultural education results from the attempts by neoconservative scholars to portray multicultural education as a movement against Western civilization, as anti-White, and by implication, anti-American (Ravitch, 1990a; Sirkin, 1990). The popular press frequently calls the movement to infuse an African perspective into the curriculum *Afrocentric,* and it has defined the term to mean an education that excludes Whites and Western civilization (Daley, 1990).

The term *Afrocentric* has different meanings to different people. Because of its diverse interpretations by various people and groups, neoconservative scholars have focused many of their criticisms of multicultural education on this concept. Asante (1987, p. 6) defines Afrocentricity as "placing African ideals at the center of any analysis that involves African culture and behavior." In other words, he defines Afro-centricity as looking at African and African American behavior from an African or African American perspective. His definition suggests that Black English, or Ebonics, cannot be understood unless it is viewed from the perspective of those who speak it. Afrocentricity, when Asante's definition is used, can describe the addition of an African American perspective to the school and university curriculum. When understood in this way, it is consistent with a multicultural curriculum because a multicultural curriculum helps students to view behavior, concepts, and issues from different ethnic and cultural perspectives.

THE CANON BATTLE: SPECIAL INTERESTS VERSUS THE PUBLIC INTEREST

The push by people of color and women to get their voices and experiences institutionalized within the curriculum and the curriculum canon transformed has evoked a strong reaction from neoconservative scholars. Consequently, a battle over the canon between people of color, feminist scholars, and neoconservative scholars is taking place. The neoconservatives have founded two organizations to resist multicultural education: the Madison Center and the National Association of Scholars. The resistance to multicultural education has been strongly expressed in a series of editorials and articles in popular and educational publications (Ravitch, 1990a, 1990b; Finn, 1990; McConnell & Breindel, 1990; Leo, 1989), as well as in several best-selling books (D'Souza, 1991; Schlesinger, 1991). The multiculturalists have founded two national organizations to defend and promote ethnic and cultural diversity in the nation's schools, colleges, and universities: Teachers for a Democratic Society and the National Association for Multicultural Education.

Many of the arguments in the editorials and articles written by the opponents of multicultural education are smoke screens for a conservative political agenda designed not to promote the common good of the nation but to reinforce the status quo, dominant group hegemony, and to promote the interests of a small elite. A clever tactic of the neoconservative scholars is to define their own interests as universal and in the public good and the interests of women and people of color as *special interests* that are particularistic (Ravitch, 1990a). When a dominant elite describes its interests as the same as the public interests, it marginalizes the experiences of structurally excluded groups, such as women and people of color.

Special interest implies an interest that is particularistic and inconsistent with the overarching goals and needs of the nation-state or commonwealth. To be in the public good, interests must extend beyond the needs of a unique or particular group. *An important issue is who formulates the criteria for determining what is a special interest.* It is the dominant group or groups in power that have already shaped the curriculum, institutions, and structures in their images and interests. The dominant group views its interests not as special but as identical with the common good. Special interests, in the view of those who control the curriculum and other institutions within society, is therefore any interest that challenges their power and dominant ideologies and paradigms, particularly if the interest group demands that the canon, assumptions, and values of the institutions and structures be transformed. History is replete with examples of dominant groups that defined their interests as the public interest.

One way in which those in power marginalize and disempower those who are structurally excluded from the mainstream is by calling their visions, histories, goals, and struggles *special interests*. This type of marginalization denies the legitimacy and validity of groups that are excluded from full participation in society and its institutions.

Only a curriculum that reflects the experiences of a wide range of groups in the United States and the world, and the interests of these groups, is in the national interest and is consistent with the public good. Any other kind of curriculum reflects a special interest and is inconsistent with the needs of a nation that must survive in a pluralistic and highly interdependent world. Special interest history and literature, such as history and literature that emphasize the primacy of the West and the history of European American males, is detrimental to the public good because it will not help students to acquire the knowledge, skills, and attitudes essential for survival in the twenty-first century.

The aim of the ethnic studies and women studies movements are not to push for special interests but to reform the curriculum so that it will be more truthful, more inclusive, and reflect the histories and experiences of the diverse groups and cultures that make up U.S. society. Rather than being special interest reform movements, they contribute to the democratization of the school and university curriculum. They contribute to the public good rather than to the strengthening of special interests.

We need to rethink concepts such as *special interests,* the *national interest,* and the *public good* and to identify which groups are using these terms and for what purposes, and to evaluate the use of these terms in the context of a nation and world that is rapidly changing. Powerless and excluded groups accurately perceive efforts to label their visions and experiences *special interests* as an attempt to marginalize them and to make their voices silent and their faces invisible.

SCHOOL KNOWLEDGE AND MULTICULTURAL LITERACY

Our concept of cultural literacy should be broader than the one presented by Hirsch (1987) in his widely reviewed book. Hirsch writes as if knowledge is neutral and static. His book contains a list of important facts that he believes students should master in order to become culturally literate. Knowledge is dynamic, changing, and constructed within a social context rather than neutral and static as Hirsch implies. Hirsch recommends transmitting knowledge in a largely uncritical way. When we help students to attain knowledge, we should help them to recognize that knowledge reflects the social context in which it is created and that it has normative and value assumptions (Banks, 1993a).

I agree with Hirsch that there is a need for all U.S. citizens to have a common core of knowledge. However, the important question is: *Who will participate in the formulation of that knowledge and whose interests will it serve?* We need a broad level of participation in the identification, construction, and formulation of the knowledge that we expect all of our citizens to master. Such knowledge should reflect cultural democracy and serve the needs of all of the people. It should contribute to public virtue and the public good. Such knowledge should not serve the needs of dominant and powerful groups, as much school and university knowledge does today. Rather, school knowledge should reflect the experiences of all of the nation's citizens and it should empower all people to participate effectively in a democratic society. It should help to empower all citizens and encourage them to participate in civic discourse and citizen action.

A TRANSFORMED CURRICULUM AND MULTIPLE PERSPECTIVES

Educators use several approaches, summarized in Figure 2–1, to integrate cultural content into the school and university curriculum (Banks, 1988a, 1991a). These include the *contributions approach,* in which content about ethnic and cultural groups are limited primarily to holidays and celebrations, such as Cinco de Mayo, Asian/Pacific Heritage Week, African American History Month, and Women's History Week. This approach is used often in the primary and elementary grades. Another frequently used approach to integrate cultural content into the curricu-

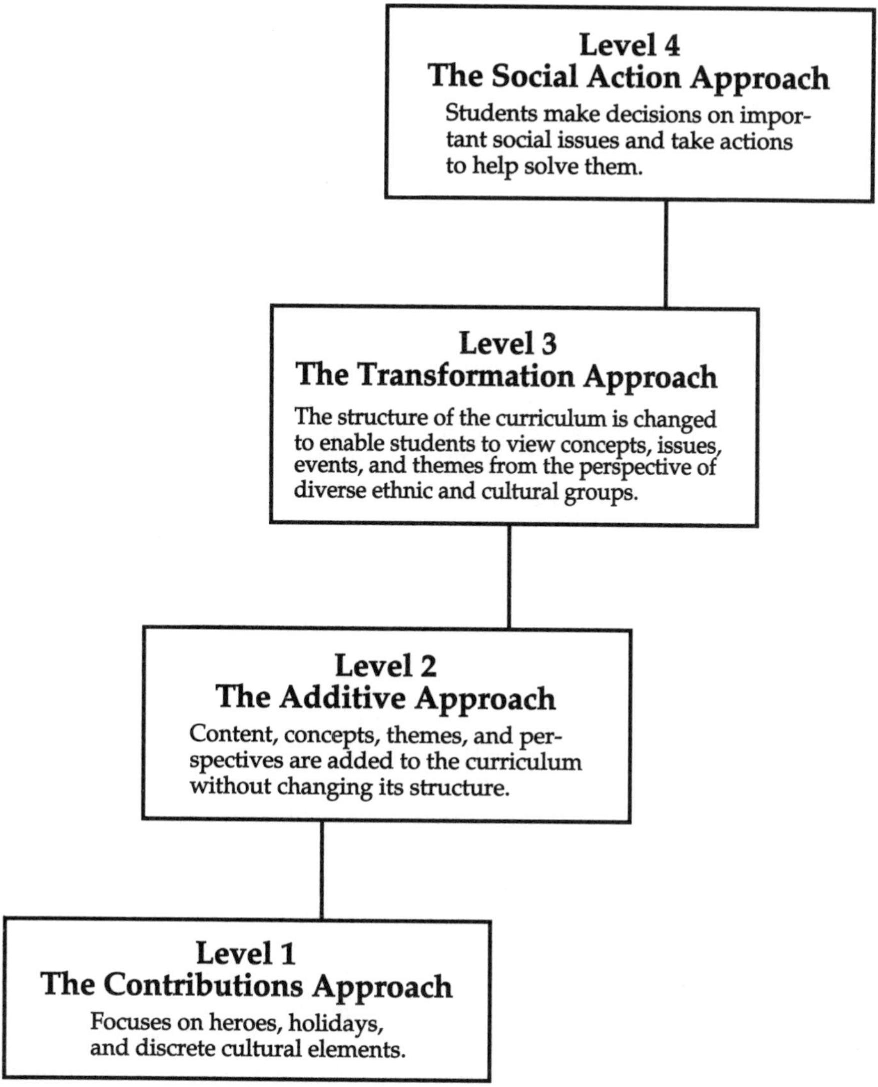

Level 4
The Social Action Approach

Students make decisions on important social issues and take actions to help solve them.

Level 3
The Transformation Approach

The structure of the curriculum is changed to enable students to view concepts, issues, events, and themes from the perspective of diverse ethnic and cultural groups.

Level 2
The Additive Approach

Content, concepts, themes, and perspectives are added to the curriculum without changing its structure.

Level 1
The Contributions Approach

Focuses on heroes, holidays, and discrete cultural elements.

FIGURE 2–1   Approaches to Multicultural Curriculum Reform

Source: Reprinted with permission from James A. Banks, "Approaches to Multicultural Curriculum Reform," *Multicultural Leader,* Vol. 1, No. 2 (Spring 1988): 1–3.

lum is the *additive approach.* In this approach, cultural content, concepts, and themes are added to the curriculum without changing its basic structure, purposes, and characteristics. The additive approach is often accomplished by the addition of a book, a unit, or a course to the curriculum without changing its framework.

Neither the contributions nor the additive approach challenges the basic structure or canon of the curriculum. Cultural celebrations, activities, and content are inserted into the curriculum within the existing curriculum framework and assumptions. When these approaches are used to integrate cultural content into the curriculum, people, events, and interpretations related to ethnic groups and women often reflect the norms and values of the dominant culture rather than those of cultural communities. Consequently, most of the ethnic groups and women added to the curriculum have values and roles consistent with those of the dominant culture. Men and women who challenged the status quo and dominant institutions are less likely to be selected for inclusion into the curriculum. Thus, Sacajawea is more likely to be chosen for inclusion than Geronimo because she helped Whites to conquer Indian lands. Geronimo resisted the takeover of Indian lands by Whites.

The *transformation approach* differs fundamentally from the contributions and additive approaches. It changes the canon, paradigms, and basic assumptions of the curriculum and enables students to view concepts, issues, themes, and problems from different perspectives and points of view. Major goals of this approach include helping students to understand concepts, events, and people from diverse ethnic and cultural perspectives and to understand knowledge as a social construction. In this approach, students are able to read and listen to the voices of the victors and the vanquished. They are also helped to analyze the teacher's perspective on events and situations and are given the opportunity to formulate and justify their own versions of events and situations. An important aim of the transformation approach is to teach students to think critically and to develop the skills to formulate, document, and justify their conclusions and generalizations.

When teaching a unit such as the "Westward Movement" using a transformation approach, the teacher would assign appropriate readings and then ask the students such questions as: What do you think the "Westward Movement" means? Who was moving West—the Whites or the Indians? What region in the United States was referred to as the West? Why? The aim of these questions is to help students to understand that the *Westward Movement* is a Eurocentric term because the Lakota Sioux were already living in the West and consequently were not moving. This phrase is used to refer to the movement of the European Americans who were headed in the direction of the Pacific Ocean. The Sioux did not consider their homeland "the West" but the center of the universe. The teacher could also ask the students to describe the Westward Movement from the point of view of the Sioux. The students might use such words as *The End, The Age of Doom,* or *The Coming of the People Who Took Our Land.* The teacher could also ask the students to give the unit a name that is more neutral than "The Westward Movement." They might name the unit "The Meeting of Two Cultures."

The *decision-making and social action approach* extends the transformative curriculum by enabling students to pursue projects and activities that allow them to take personal, social, and civic actions related to the concepts, problems, and issues they have studied. After they have studied the unit on different perspectives on the Westward Movement, the students might decide that they want to learn more about American Indians and to take actions that will enable the school to depict and perpetuate more accurate and positive views of America's first inhabitants. The students might compile a list of books written by American Indians for the school librarian to order, and present a pageant for the school's morning exercise on "The Westward Movement: A View from the Other Side."

TEACHING STUDENTS TO KNOW, TO CARE, AND TO ACT

Major goals of a transformative curriculum that fosters multicultural literacy should be to help students *to know, to care, and to act* in ways that will develop and foster a democratic and just society in which all groups experience cultural democracy and cultural empowerment. Knowledge is an essential part of multicultural literacy but it is not sufficient. Knowledge alone will not help students to develop an empathetic, caring, commitment to humane and democratic change. An essential goal of a multicultural curriculum is to help students to develop empathy and caring. To help our nation and world become more culturally democratic, students must also develop a commitment to personal, social, and civic action, and the knowledge and skills needed to participate in effective civic action.

Although knowledge, caring, and action are conceptually distinct, in the classroom they are highly interrelated. In my multicultural classes for teacher education students, I use historical and sociological knowledge about the experiences of different ethnic and racial groups to inform as well as to enable the students to examine and clarify their personal attitudes about ethnic diversity. These knowledge experiences are also a vehicle that enables the students to think of action they can take to actualize their feelings and moral commitments.

Knowledge experiences that I use to help students to examine their value commitments and to think of ways to act include the reading of *Balm in Gilead: Journey of a Healer*, Sara Lawrence Lightfoot's (1988) powerful biography of her mother, one of the nation's first African American child psychiatrists; the historical overviews of various U.S. ethnic groups in my book, *Teaching Strategies for Ethnic Studies* (Banks, 1991a); and several video and film presentations, including selected segments from *Eyes on the Prize II,* the award-winning history of the Civil Rights Movement produced by Henry Hampton, and *Eye of the Beholder,* a powerful videotape that uses simulation to show the cogent effects of discrimination on adults. The videotape features Jane Elliott, who attained fame for her well-known experiment in which she discriminated against children on the basis of skin color to teach them about discrimination (Peters, 1987).

To enable the students to analyze and clarify their values regarding these readings and video experiences, I ask them questions such as: How did the book, film, or videotape make you feel? Why do you think you feel that way? To enable them to think about ways to act on their feelings, I ask such questions as: How interracial are your own personal experiences? Would you like to live a more interracial life? What are some books that you can read or popular films that you can see that will enable you to act on your commitment to live a more racially and ethnically integrated life? The power of these kinds of experiences are often revealed in student papers, as is illustrated by this excerpt from a paper written by a student after he had viewed several segments of *Eyes on the Prize II* (Muir, 1990):

> *I feel that my teaching will now necessarily be a little bit different forever simply because I myself have changed. . . . I am no longer quite the same person I was before I viewed the presentations—my horizons are a little wider, perspectives a little broader, insights a little deeper. That is what I gained from* Eyes on the Prize.

The most meaningful and effective way to prepare teachers to involve students in multicultural experiences that will enable students to know, to care, and to participate in democratic action is to involve teachers in multicultural experiences that focus on these goals. When teachers have gained knowledge about cultural and ethnic diversity themselves, looked at that knowledge from different ethnic and cultural perspectives, and taken action to make their own lives and communities more culturally sensitive and diverse, they will have the knowledge and skills needed to help transform the curriculum canon as well the hearts and minds of their students. Only when the curriculum canon is transformed to reflect cultural diversity will students in our schools and colleges be able to attain the knowledge, skills, and perspectives needed to participate effectively in the global society of the next century.

MULTICULTURAL EDUCATION AND
NATIONAL SURVIVAL

Multicultural education is needed to help all of the nation's future citizens to acquire the knowledge, attitudes, and skills needed to survive in the twenty-first century. Nothing less than the nation's survival is at stake. The rapid growth in the nation's population of people of color, the escalating importance of non-White nations such as China and Japan, and the widening gap between the rich and the poor make it essential for our future citizens to have multicultural literacy and cross-cultural skills. In the twenty-first century, a nation whose citizens cannot negotiate on the world's multicultural global stage will not only be tremendously disadvantaged but its very survival may be imperiled.

3

SCHOOL REFORM AND INTERGROUP EDUCATION

Teachers and administrators for schools of today and tomorrow should acquire the knowledge, attitudes, and skills needed to work with students from diverse cultural groups and to help all students develop more positive racial attitudes. Teachers and administrators also need to restructure schools so that they will be able to deal effectively with the nation's growing diversity and to prepare future citizens who will be able to compete in a global world economy that will be knowledge and service oriented.

The first part of this chapter describes the demographic trends and developments related to the nation's changing ethnic texture and future workforce, states why school restructuring is essential in order to prepare the workforce needed for tomorrow, and describes the major variables of multicultural school reform.

The second part describes the characteristics of children's racial attitudes and guidelines for helping students to acquire more positive racial attitudes, values, beliefs, and actions. This knowledge is essential for the preparation of teachers and administrators who will practice in twenty-first century schools.

DEMOGRAPHIC TRENDS AND THE CHANGING WORKFORCE

The U.S. workforce faces several major problems as we enter the twenty-first century that have important implications for the professional work of teachers and administrators. Teachers and administrators need to be aware of these trends and to take part in school reform efforts designed to restructure our schools and institutions of higher education so that they will be able to respond to these demographic trends sensitively and reflectively. I call these trends the *demographic imperative.*

As we enter the twenty-first century, the nation will have a large number of people retiring and too few new workers entering the workforce. Our population is also becoming increasingly older. In 1980, about 12.5 percent of the nation's population consisted of people over age 65. By 2030, 22 percent of the nation's population will be in that age group (Richman, 1990). The cost of supporting older workers will continue to mount as we move toward the next century. We will be dependent on fewer workers to support every retiree. In the boom years of the 1950s, 17 workers supported every retiree. The ratio now is about 3 workers to 1 retiree. Out of about every 3 of these workers is a person of color (Hodgkinson, 1985). If the education of students of color does not improved significantly and quickly, a large number of the workers depended on to contribute to the incomes of retired workers will not have the skills and knowledge to participate effectively in a workforce that will be knowledge and service oriented.

The nation's economy is becoming increasingly global. Foreign investment in the United States grew from $90 billion in 1980 to $304.2 billion in 1988 (U.S. Companies, 1989). The United States, as well as the other modernized nations, have moved from agricultural, to industrial, to knowledge/service societies. Bell (1973) calls these kinds of societies *post-industrial;* Toffler (1980) calls them *third wave.* Workers in the twenty-first century must have the knowledge, attitudes, and skills needed to compete in a global world economy that is primarily service oriented. All of the new jobs and most of the new wealth created between now and the turn of the century will be in service industries (Johnson & Packer, 1987). U.S. employers will not limit their search for skilled knowledge workers to the boundaries of this nation. U.S. workers will have to compete with skilled knowledge workers throughout the world.

People of color will constitute a disproportionate share of the workforce in the next century. Between 1980 and 2000, about 83 percent of the new entrants to the labor force will be either women, people of color, or immigrants. Native White males will make up only 15 percent of the new entrants to the labor force during this period (Johnson & Packer, 1987). *As we enter the 21st century—if current trends continue—there will be a mismatch between the knowledge and skills demands of the workforce, and the knowledge and skills of a large proportion of U.S. workers.* About one-third of these workers will be people of color.

Workforce Needs in the Twenty-First Century

Knowledge-oriented service jobs, in fields such as education, health, and trade, will require high-level reasoning and analytical, quantitative, and communication skills. Most corporations in the next century, like many today, will have a transnational identity and will find skilled workers to complete required jobs in any nation or part of the world, and not within a particular nation, such as the United States.

In a segment of the PBS series, "Learning in America," it was revealed that a New York insurance company was sending paperwork by plane to Dublin at regular intervals to be done by workers there because the company regarded these workers as more competent than comparable workers in the United States. This U.S. insurance company was sending work to Dublin to be done at the same time that the unemployment rate among African American teenagers was as high as 30 to 40 percent in some inner-city communities.

The sending of work to Dublin by an American insurance company foreshadows a trend that is likely to escalate in the future and pose serious problems for the development of productive U.S. citizens among ethnic groups of color in the United States. As we move further into the twenty-first century, there will be an increasing need for highly skilled and technical workers in the United States and throughout the world. Yet, if the current levels of educational attainments among most U.S. youths of color continues, the nation will be hard pressed to meet its labor needs with its own citizens. In 1990, 32.4 percent of Hispanic youths and 13.2 percent of African American youths between the ages of 16 and 24 had dropped out of high school, compared to 9 percent of White youths and 12 percent of all youths (U.S. Bureau of the Census, 1992, p. 160).

There will be a mismatch between the skills of a large percentage of the workers in the United States and the needs of the labor force. Writes Richman (1990, p. 74):

> *A terrifying gap looms between the skills that employers need and the training that this new workforce will have received. The Bureau of Labor Statistics estimates that jobs requiring a college degree will rise from 22% of the total to 30% by the end of the century. However, college enrollment among African American youth declined 7% in the past decade. Among Hispanics, the fastest-growing group of new labor force entrants, the high school drop-out rate is 40 percent, triple the national average.*

Scientific, technical, and service jobs will be ample, but the potential workers—about one-third of whom will be people of color—will not have the knowledge and skills to do the jobs. This will occur because of the increasingly large percentage of the school-age population that will be youths of color by 2020 (about 46 percent) and the low quality of the elementary and secondary education that a large number of youths of color are receiving. The problems that these students experience in the schools are summarized in the report, *Education that Works* (Quality Education for Minorities Project, 1990, pp. 11–12), a report published at Massachusetts Institute of Technology:

> *Many schools . . . continue to operate with outmoded curricula and structures based on the assumption that only a small elite will have or need to have substantial academic success. The problems our children face in and out of the classroom—racism, poverty, language differences, and cultural barriers—are not adequately addressed in today's typical school. We have had, consequently, low achievement and high dropout rates.*

There will be an insufficient number of Whites, and particularly White males, to meet U.S. labor demands in the early years of the next century. Consequently, to meet workforce demands in the early years of the next century, women and people of color will have to enter scientific and technical fields in greater numbers. One out of three Ph.D.s awarded in the natural sciences and engineering in 1988 went to foreigners, compared with one in four in 1977. *Time* magazine wrote in its September 11, 1989, issue, "The science deficit threatens America's prosperity and possibly even its national security."

Whites are a diminishing percentage of new entrants to the U.S. labor force and of the nation's population because of the low birthrate among Whites and the small proportion of immigrants to the United States that are coming from Europe. Between 1981 and 1986, about 85 percent of the documented immigrants to the United States came from Latin America (38 percent) and Asia (47 percent); only 11 percent came from Europe.

The United States is experiencing its largest wave of immigrants since the turn of the last century when many Southern, Eastern, and Central European immigrants came to this land. About 600,000 documented and 200,000 undocumented immigrants enter the United States each year. Because of the low birthrate among Whites, the large influx of immigrants from Asia and Latin America, and the high birthrates among these groups, the White percentage of the U.S. population is experiencing very little growth. The White population in the United States grew about 2 percent between 1980 and 1988, compared to about 12 percent for African Americans, over 30 percent for Hispanics, and over 55 percent for Asians (Henry, 1990, p. 30). Hispanics are one of the nation's fastest growing groups. They increased from about 14 million in 1980 to more than 20 million in 1990 (Banks, 1991a).

Today, about one of every four Americans is a person of color. By the turn of the century, if current growth trends continue, one-third of all Americans will be persons of color (Commission on Minority Participation, 1988). The growth in the nation's percentage of people of color is expected to outpace the growth in the percentage of Whites into the foreseeable future. In its April 9, 1990, issue (Henry, 1990), *Time* magazine stated that by the year 2056, Whites may be a minority group in the United States if present trends continue. This projection is tenuous and premature. It may also unnecessarily inflame nativism and xenophobia.

The Problem of Poverty and the Development of the Future Workforce

The gap between the relatively affluent 85 percent of U.S. society and the desperately poor 15 percent of the population continues to widen (Staff of *Fortune,* 1990). This gap is divided heavily along racial lines. While the percentage of Whites living below the official U.S. government poverty line decreased during the last eight years, the percentage of African Americans and Hispanics living in poverty increased. Many African Americans and Hispanics are trapped in low-income inner-city communities in which they not only have little contact with Whites, but they also have little contact and interaction with middle- and upper-status members of their own ethnic groups (Wilson, 1987).

The desertion of inner-city communities is not by Whites alone. Middle-class African Americans and Hispanics have joined the exodus to the suburbs and to private schools. A salient characteristic of the United States today is a deepening social-class schism within as well as across ethnic and racial groups. Today, the flight out of the inner-city is class as well as racial. Consequently, a large group of low-income African American and Hispanic youths are socialized within communities in which they have little contact and interaction with middle-class individuals who belong to their own ethnic groups.

These youths are often called *the underclass* by the popular media and social scientists. This term is considered pejorative by many people and may contribute to the further marginalization of these youths and their families.

Prior to the Civil Rights Movement of the 1960s and 1970s, and the open housing legislation that resulted from it, most middle-class African Americans and Hispanics professionals, such as teachers, lawyers, and social workers, lived in ethnic communities and served as important role models, mentors, and inspirational leaders for low-income ethnic youths. These ethnic professionals were confined to ethnic communities largely because of housing discrimination.

An increasing percentage of the nation's school-age youths are victims of poverty as well as confined and isolated in low-income inner-city communities. About one of every five children in the United States lives in poverty (Ford Foundation, 1989, p. 10). The proportion of children living in poverty is expected to increase in the years ahead, from about 21 percent of all children in 1984 to 27 percent of all children in 2020 (Pallas, Natriello, & McDill, 1989). The large number of American youths who are victims of poverty poses a serious problem for the development of effective citizens and workers. Youths who are victims of poverty are at a high risk of becoming school dropouts, experiencing academic failure, and engaging in antisocial behavior. It is very difficult for youths who drop out of school or who experience academic failure to become effective and productive citizens in a postindustrial, knowledge society.

Restructuring Schools

An important implication of the demographic and social trends described above is that a major goal of education must be to help low-income students, linguistic minority students, and students of color to develop the knowledge, attitudes, and skills needed to participate in the mainstream workforce and in the mainstream society in the twenty-first century. This goal is essential but is not sufficient—nor is it possible to attain, in my view, without restructuring educational institutions and institutionalizing new goals and ideals within them. We must also rethink the goals of our society and nation-state if we are to enter the twenty-first century as a strong, democratic, and just society.

I do not believe that our schools, as they are currently structured, conceptualized, and organized, will be able to help most students of color and linguistic minority students—especially those who are poor and from cultures that differ from the school culture in significant ways—to acquire the knowledge, attitudes, and skills needed to function effectively in the knowledge society of the next century. Our schools were designed for a different population at a time when immigrant and poor youths did not need to be literate or have basic skills to get jobs and to become self-supporting citizens. When large numbers of immigrants entered the United States at the turn of the century, jobs in heavy industry were available that required little knowledge or skills. Thus, the school was less important as a job-preparatory institution.

To help our future citizens become effective and productive citizens in the next century, our schools must be restructured. *By restructuring, I mean a fundamental examination of the goals, values, and purposes of schools and a reconstruction of them.* When restructuring occurs, the total system is recognized as the problem and is the target of reform. Incremental and piecemeal changes are viewed as insufficient as a reform strategy.

To restructure schools, we need educational leaders who have a vision and who are transformative in orientation. In his influential book, *Leadership,* Burns (1978) identifies two types of leaders: *transformative* and *transactional.* Transformative leaders have a vision that they use to mobilize people to action. This is in contrast to transactional leadership. This type of leadership is quid pro quo: "If you scratch my back, I will scratch yours." Transactional leadership, which is pervasive within our educational institutions and the larger society, is not motivating people to act and is not resulting in the kinds of changes that we need to respond to the demographic imperative I have described above. To respond to the demographic imperative, we need transformative leaders with a vision of the future and who have the skills and abilities to communicate that vision to others.

Schools must help youths from diverse cultures and groups to attain the knowledge, attitudes, and skills needed to function effectively in the twenty-first century. To attain this goal, the school must change many of its basic assumptions and practices. School restructuring is essential because the dominant approaches, techniques, and practices used to educate students do not, and I believe will not, succeed with large numbers of students of color, such as African Americans, Native Americans, and Hispanics. Most current school practices are having little success with these students for many complex reasons, including negative perceptions and expectations of them that are held by many teachers and administrators. Many of the adults in the lives of these students have little faith in their ability, and many of the students—who have internalized these negative views—have little faith in themselves.

Many of these students are socialized in families and communities where they have seen a lot of failure, misery, and disillusionment. Many of them have seen or experienced little success, especially success that is related to schooling and education. One high school teacher asked a group of his students to write about their successes and failures. One of his Native American students told him that he could not write about success but that he could write easily and at length about failure because he had experienced so much of it. The student wrote a poignant and moving essay about the daunting failures that he had experienced in his short life.

Increasing Academic Achievement

To help students of color and poor students to experience academic success, and thus to become effective citizens, the school must be restructured so that these students will have successful experiences within a nurturing, personalized, and caring environment. Some fundamental reforms will have to occur in schools for this kind of environment to be created. Grouping practices that relegate a disproportionate number of low-income students and students of color to lower-tracked classes in which they receive an inferior education will have to be dismantled (Oakes, 1992). A norm will have to be institutionalized within the school that states that all students can and will learn, regardless of their home situations, race, social class, or ethnic group.

The theories and techniques developed by researchers such as Ronald Edmonds (1986) and James Comer (1988) can help schools bring about the structural changes needed to implement the idea within a school that all children can and will learn. Innovative ways will need to be devised that will involve a joint parent-school effort in the education of ethnic and linguistic minority students. Most parents want their children to experience success in school, even though they may have neither the knowledge nor the resources to actualize their aspirations for their children. Successful educational interventions with low-income students and students of color are more likely to succeed if they have a parent-involvement component, as Comer (1988) has demonstrated with his successful interventions in inner-city, predominantly Black schools. Because of the tremendous changes that have occurred in U.S. families within the last two decades, we need to rethink and reconceptualize what parent involvement means and to formulate new ways to involve parents at a time when large numbers of school-age youths are from single-parent or two-working parent families (C. A. M. Banks, 1993).

Empowering Teachers

To restructure schools in a way that increase their ability to educate low-income youths and youths of color, classroom teachers must be nurtured, empowered, and revitalized. Disempowered, alienated, underpaid, and disaffected teachers cannot help students who are victimized by poverty and discrimination to master the knowledge and skills they need to participate effectively in the mainstream society in the twenty-first century.

Many of the teachers in U.S. schools—especially those who work in inner-city schools with large numbers of low-income students, students of color, and linguistic minority students—are victimized by societal forces similar to those that victimize their students. Many of these teachers are underpaid, held in low esteem by elites in society, treated with little respect by the bureaucratic and hierarchial school districts in which they work, victims of stereotypes, and blamed for many problems that are beyond their control.

It is unreasonable to expect disempowered and victimized teachers to empower and motivate disaffected youths of color. *Consequently, a major goal of school restructuring must be to give teachers respect, the ability to make decisions that matter, and to hold them accountable as professionals for the decisions they make.* School reform will succeed only if we treat teachers in ways that we have long admonished them to treat their students. We must have high expectations for teachers, involve them genuinely in decision-making, stop teacher bashing, and treat teachers in a caring and humane way. Only when teachers feel empowered and honored will they have the will and ability to treat students that society has victimized with respect and caring.

The Need for Societal Reform

Teachers and administrators should have the knowledge and skills needed to help students to become change agents within society. Education should not just educate students to fit into the existing workforce and the current societal structure. Citizenship education in a multicultural society should have as an important goal helping all students to develop the knowledge, attitudes, and skills needed to participate within but also to help reform and reconstruct our society. Problems such as racism, sexism, poverty, and inequality are widespread within U.S. society and permeate many of the nation's institutions, such as the workforce, the courts, and the schools. To educate future citizens merely to fit into and not to change society will result in a perpetuation and escalation of these problems, including the widening gap between the rich and the poor, racial conflict and tension, and the growing number of people who are victims of poverty and homelessness.

A society that has sharp divisions between the rich and the poor, and between Whites and people of color, is not a stable one. It contains stresses and tensions that can lead to societal upheavals and racial polarization and conflict. Thus, education for the twenty-first century must not only help students to become literate and reflective citizens who can participate productively in the workforce but it must also teach them to care about other people in their communities and to take personal, social, and civic action to create a more humane and just society.

AMERICA'S FUTURE

The demographic trends and projections described above indicate that the United States must act quickly to educate its low-income population and to preserve its rich linguistic and cultural resources, or face the future as a second-rate and declining nation. This is because the White population is aging and declining as a percentage of the population, while the population of people of color—especially Asians and Hispanics—is growing by leaps and bounds. In the future, Whites will make up a disproportionate share of the nation's retirees, who will be heavily dependent on workers of color to support them through the Social Security benefit system.

America's poor children, children of color, and linguistic minority students are an important part of its future. America's ultimate test as a nation will be not how it treats its citizens who are successful but how it responds to the desperate plight of those who are poor and undereducated. These citizens have the potential to help the nation enter the twenty-first century with strength and compassion. There are some hopeful signs that an increasing number of Americans are beginning to realize that bold steps must be taken to educate its citizens of color and to educate all of its citizens to live in a multicultural society, not out of kindness for the downtrodden, but for national survival.

INTERGROUP EDUCATION

The first part of this chapter focused on the need for school reform to increase the academic achievement of all students, especially the achievement of ethnic minority and low-income youth who experience many academic problems. Another important goal of multicultural education is to reduce prejudice among all students and to help them to develop more democratic attitudes, beliefs, and actions. This section describes the nature of children's racial attitudes and guidelines for helping students to develop positive racial attitudes, beliefs, and actions.

The Nature of Children's Racial Attitudes and Identity

Teachers of young children often tell me that their students are not aware of racial differences and have no racial prejudices. However, research over a period that spans more than 60 years indicates that young children are aware of the racial differences within adult society. Their racial attitudes mirror those of adults (Lasker, 1929; Cross, 1991).

In a series of landmark studies published between 1939 and 1950, Kenneth and Mamie Clark (1939, 1950), working with African Americans aged 3 to 7, established a paradigm in racial attitude research that is still highly influential. Using brown and white dolls as stimuli, the Clarks established that young African American children have accurate knowledge about different racial groups, tend to prefer white to brown dolls, and often make incorrect racial self-identifications. The Clarks interpreted the tendency by African American children to prefer white to brown dolls and to make incorrect racial self-identifications as expressions of negative self-esteem, low self-concept, identity confusion, and racial self-rejection.

During the 1950s and 1960s, a score of other researchers—working within the research paradigm established by the Clarks—confirmed the Clarks' findings (e.g., Goodman, 1952; Williams & Edwards, 1969). Most of this research also included preschool and kindergarten White children as subjects. It indicated that White children tend to make own-group preferences (tend to select White dolls) and, unlike African American children, tend to make correct racial self-identifications.

The Clarks' paradigm, which may be called the *self-rejection hypothesis,* dominated the social science and educational literature from the 1930s to the 1970s. Since the 1970s, however, the Clarks' paradigm has been seriously challenged by a number of researchers and theorists. The challenges to the Clarks' paradigm have taken several forms, including the search for different explanations of the pro-white bias exemplified by African American children, a few studies that have contradicted their findings, and arguments that describe the methodological weaknesses of the studies by the Clarks and their followers.

During the 1980s, researchers such as Spencer (1982, 1984) and Cross (1991) developed concepts, theories, and research that strongly challenged the notion that young African American children who express Eurocentric racial preferences have negative self-esteem, self-hate, and dysfunctional personalities. These researchers have made a useful conceptual distinction between *personal identity* (self-concept, self-esteem) and *group identity* or *reference group* orientation. In a series of pioneering studies, Spencer (1982, 1984) has marshaled significant support for the postulate that young African American children are able to distinguish their *personal identity* from their *group identity,* can have high self-esteem and yet express a White bias, and that the expression of a White bias results from a *cognitive process* that enables young children to accurately perceive the norms and attitudes toward Whites and Blacks in American society.

Banks and Banks (1983) studied the racial attitudes, preferences, and self-identifications of a sample of 23 preschool and kindergarten African

American children who lived in the predominantly White suburban communities of a city in the Northwest. The children in this study had *biracial* attitudes. They liked both African Americans and Whites. Most of them believed that Blacks and Whites were equally good looking and equally good as students. However, they were slightly biased toward African Americans.

Previous investigators have assumed that psychologically healthy children should make own-group racial preferences. They have assumed this in large part because most White children, beginning at age 4, make own-group racial preferences. African American and Mexican American children tend to make in-group as well as out-group racial preferences, which I call *biracial* or *bicultural* preferences. Parents of color tend to socialize their children so that they will function effectively both in their ethnic communities and in the mainstream society.

There is almost no discussion in existing studies of the extent to which young children make *biracial* choices. These findings tend to be ignored or to be interpreted negatively because they are inconsistent with existing research paradigms. We live in a multicultural society. A research paradigm needs to be established that focuses on the bicultural and biracial choices that children make, that interprets the important differences within ethnic groups, and that assumes that bigroup preferences, rather than own-group preferences, are healthy and desirable within a multicultural society.

The Modification of Children's Racial Attitudes

In a comprehensive review of the research (Banks, 1993b), I identify four types of intervention studies that have been conducted to help children to develop more democratic racial attitudes and behaviors. These are *laboratory reinforcement* studies, *perceptual differentiation* studies, *curricular intervention* studies, and studies that use *cooperative learning* activities and contact situations. This research indicates that teachers can help students to develop more positive racial attitudes by designing and implementing well-planned and well-conceptualized curricular interventions.

In a series of laboratory studies conducted by Williams and Morland (1976) and their colleagues, researchers have been able to reduce White bias in both African American and White children by using reinforcement procedures. In one study (Williams & Edwards, 1969), for example, the investigators showed the children a white horse and a black horse, and a white figure and a brown figure. The researchers were able to reduce White bias in the students by giving them positive reinforcement when they chose positive—rather than negative—adjectives to describe the black horse and the brown figure. Researchers using reinforcement techniques have found that when White bias is reduced using black and white animals and boxes, the changed attitudes are generalized to human figures and photographs. *It is important to point out that these interventions reduce but do not eliminate White bias in young children.*

Katz and Zalk (1978) examined the effects of four different interventions on the racial attitudes of second- and fifth-grade children high in prejudice. The four interventions were: perceptual differentiation of minority group faces, increased positive interracial contact, vicarious interracial contact, and reinforcement of the color black. The perceptual differentiation treatment was based on the hypothesis that people find it more difficult to differentiate the faces of members of out-groups than to differentiate the faces of members of their own groups. It is not uncommon to hear a member of one racial group say that he or she has trouble telling members of another group apart. Katz and Zalk hypothesized that if they could teach children to better differentiate the faces of out-groups, prejudice would be reduced. Each of the four interventions was effective in reducing prejudice. However, the *vicarious contact* and *perceptual differentiation* treatments had the most long-term effects.

A number of curriculum intervention studies that use multiethnic materials have been conducted. Trager and Yarrow (1952) found that first- and second-grade children who experienced a democratic, multicultural curriculum developed more positive racial attitudes than students who experienced a traditional, mainstream curriculum. Litcher and Johnson (1969) found that multiethnic readers helped White, second-grade children to develop more positive racial attitudes. However, when they replicated the study using photographs (Litcher, Johnson, and Ryan, 1973), the children's attitudes were not significantly changed. The Litcher, Johnson, and Ryan study highlights an important trend in the prejudice-reduction literature. Although curricular materials can help students develop more positive racial attitudes, successful intervention is a complicated process that is influenced by a number of factors, including the teacher's racial attitudes and skills, the length of the intervention, the classroom atmosphere, the ethnic and racial composition of the school and classroom, and the racial atmosphere and composition of the community.

Since 1970, a number of researchers have studied the effects of cooperative learning on the academic achievement and racial attitudes of students from different racial and ethnic groups (Aronson & Gonzalez, 1988; Slavin, 1983). This research has been heavily influenced by the theory developed by Allport (1954). Allport hypothesized that prejudice would be reduced if interracial contact situations have the following characteristics:

1. They are cooperative rather than competitive.
2. The individuals experience equal status.
3. The individuals have shared goals.
4. The contact is sanctioned by authorities such as parents, principals, and teachers.

The research on cooperative learning activities indicate that African American, Mexican American, and White students develop more positive racial attitudes and choose more friends from outside racial groups when they participate in group activities that have the conditions identified by Allport. Cooperative learning activities also have a positive effect on the academic achievement of students of color.

GUIDELINES FOR REDUCING PREJUDICE IN STUDENTS

The following guidelines are derived from the research discussed above as well as from two recent reviews that I have completed (Banks, 1991, Banks, 1993b):

1. *Include positive and realistic images of ethnic and racial groups in teaching materials in a consistent, natural, and integrated fashion.*
2. *Help children to differentiate the faces of members of outside racial and ethnic groups.* The best way to do this is to permeate the curriculum with different faces of members of these groups.
3. *Involve children in vicarious experiences with various racial and ethnic groups.* For example, use films, videos, children's books, recordings, photographs, and other kinds of vicarious experiences to expose children to members of different racial and ethnic groups. Vicarious experiences are especially important for students in predominantly White, Latino, or African American schools or communities who do not have much direct contact with members of other racial, ethnic, and social-class groups. Research indicates that vicarious experiences can be powerful (Katz & Zalk, 1978; Litcher & Johnson, 1969). However, vicarious experiences with different ethnic and racial groups should acquaint students with many different types of people within these groups.

4. *If you teach in an interracial school, involve children in structured inter-racial contact situations.* However, contact alone does not necessarily help children to develop positive racial attitudes. Effective interracial contact situations must have the characteristics described by Allport (1954).

5. *Provide positive verbal and nonverbal reinforcement for the color brown.*

6. *Involve children from different racial and ethnic groups in cooperative learning activities.*

Preparing Students for a Changing, Diverse, and Troubled World

The demographic changes that are taking place in the United States make it essential for teachers and administrators to: (1) restructure schools so that students from all ethnic, racial, gender, and social-class groups will have an equal opportunity to learn; and (2) implement prejudice-reduction strategies so that all students will develop the knowledge, attitudes, and skills needed to function is an increasingly diverse, tense, and problem-ridden world. Because of the enormous problems within our nation and world, educators cannot be neutral (Edelman, 1992). They can either act to help transform our world or enhance the escalation of our problems by inaction. Each educator must make a choice. What will be yours?

4

KNOWLEDGE COMPONENTS

Eight characteristics of the multicultural school were described in Chapter 1 (See Table 1–2). Each of these elements must be reformed in schools in order to enable them to create equal educational opportunities for all students and to help students develop the knowledge, skills, and attitudes needed to function effectively in a changing national and world society. One of the eight characteristics of an effective multicultural school identified in Table 1–2 is positive teacher attitudes and behaviors. To acquire the attitudes, perceptions, and behavior needed to actualize multicultural education in their schools, teachers need a sound knowledge base in multicultural education. This chapter describes the knowledge teachers need to become effective in multicultural classrooms and schools.

THE FOUR KNOWLEDGE CATEGORIES

To become effective multicultural teachers, teachers need the following:

1. *Knowledge of the major paradigms* in multicultural education
2. *Knowledge of the major concepts* in multicultural education
3. *Historical and cultural knowledge* of the major ethnic groups
4. *Pedagogical knowledge* about how to adapt curriculum and instruction to the unique needs of students from diverse cultural, ethnic, and social-class groups

This chapter focuses on the first three categories of knowledge named above. Chapter 5 describes pedagogical knowledge.

MULTICULTURAL EDUCATION PARADIGMS

A paradigm is an interrelated set of ideas that explain human behavior or a phenomenon. It implies policy and action and has specific goals, assumptions, and values. Paradigms compete with one another in the arena of ideas and public policy.

Since the 1960s, several major paradigms have been formulated explaining why many low-income and ethnic minority students have low levels of academic achievement (Banks, 1994). Two of these paradigms or explanations are the *cultural deprivation* paradigm and the *cultural difference* paradigm. These two paradigms have very different assumptions, research findings, and implications for teaching in multicultural classrooms. Teachers who embrace the cultural deprivation paradigm and those who embrace the cultural difference paradigm are likely to respond to minority students differently in classroom interactions and to have different ideas about how to increase the academic achievement of minority and low-income students. See Banks (1994) for a discussion of other paradigms. A fuller discussion of the two discussed here follows.

The Cultural Deprivation Paradigm

Cultural deprivation theorists assume that low-income students do not achieve well in school because of the culture of poverty in which they are socialized. They believe that characteristics such as poverty, disorganized families, and single-parent homes cause children from low-income communities to experience "cultural deprivation" and "irreversible cognitive deficits."

Cultural deprivationists assume that a major goal of the school is to provide "culturally deprived" children with the cultural and other experiences that will compensate for their cognitive and intellectual deficits. These theorists believe that low-income students can learn the basic skills taught by the schools, but these skills must be taught by using intensive behaviorist teaching techniques.

Cultural deprivation theorists see the major problem as the culture of the students rather than the culture of the school. Teachers and administrators who embrace the cultural deprivation paradigm often "blame the victims" for their problems and academic failure. They assume that low-income and students of color often do poorly in school because of their cultural and social-class characteristics, not because they are ineffectively taught. They believe that the school is limited in what it can do to help these students achieve because of the culture into which they are socialized. Advocates of this paradigm focus on changing the student rather than changing the culture of the school to enable it to focus on the cultural strengths of students from diverse social-class and ethnic groups.

The Cultural Difference Paradigm

Unlike the cultural deprivation theorists, cultural difference theorists reject the idea that ethnic minority students have cultural deficits. They believe that ethnic groups such as African Americans, Mexican Americans, Asian Americans, and Native Americans have strong, rich, and diverse cultures. These cultures consist of languages, values, behavioral styles, and perspectives that can enrich the lives of all Americans. Ethnic minority youths fail to achieve in school not because they have culturally deprived cultures but because their cultures are different from the culture of the school.

Cultural difference theorists believe that the school, rather than the cultures of minority students, is primarily responsible for the low academic achievement of minority students. The school must change in ways that will allow it to respect and reflect the cultures of minority students and at the same time use teaching strategies that are consistent with their cultural characteristics. Culturally sensitive and enriched teaching strategies will motivate low-income and minority students and enable them to achieve at high levels. The schools, argue cultural difference theorists, often fail to help ethnic minority students to achieve because schools frequently ignore or try to alienate them from their cultures, and rarely use teaching strategies that are consistent with their life-styles. Cultural difference theorists frequently cite research that shows how the culture of the school and the cultures of ethnic minority students differ in values, norms, and behaviors (Ramírez & Castañeda, 1974; Heath, 1983).

Much of the research developed by cultural difference theorists focus on the language and learning style of students of color. Linguists such as Roger Shuy, William Labov, and Joan Baratz (Williams, 1970) have described Black English, or Ebonics (the dialect of English spoken by many African Americans) as a rich version of English that is logical, consistent in style and usage, and very effective in communicating a sense of kinship and unity among African Americans. Many teachers, however, view Black English negatively. Sociolinguists urge teachers to view Black English from a positive perspective and to use it as a vehicle to help its speakers to learn Standard English as an alternative dialect, not as a replacement for their first language. Cultural difference theorists also advise teachers to view other languages spoken by their students, such as Spanish and Vietnamese, as strengths rather than as problems to be overcome (Minami & Kennedy, 1992; Ovando & Collier, 1985).

Research by cultural difference theorists such as Hale-Benson (1986), Shade (1982), Ramírez and Castañeda (1974), Philips (1983), Vogt, Jordan, and Tharp (1987), Delpit (1988), Irvine (1990), and Ladson-Billings (1990) indicate that most African American, Hispanic, Native American, and Native Hawaiian students have some learning and cultural characteristics that are inconsistent with the school culture.

This research indicates, for example, that Mexican American students tend to be more field-sensitive than mainstream White students. Field-sensitive and field-independent students differ in behavior and characteristics. Field-sensitive students tend to like to work with others to achieve a common goal. They are more sensitive to the feelings and opinions of others than are field-independent students. Field-independent students prefer to work independently and to compete and gain individual recognition.

Research on the effects of cooperative learning techniques by Slavin (1983) and Aronson and Gonzalez (1988) supports the theories of the learning styles advocates. These researchers have found that the academic achievement of minority students are enhanced when they are taught using cooperative learning strategies. This research also indicates that both White and ethnic minority students develop more positive racial attitudes when they participate in cooperative learning situations.

CONCEPTS IN MULTICULTURAL EDUCATION

Concepts are important ideas that scientists use to classify and categorize information, data, and ideas (see Chapter 5). The heart of a discipline or field of study is its key concepts, generalizations, and principles. Culture is a major concept in multicultural education. We will now examine culture and two related concepts: macroculture and microculture.

Culture

There are many different definitions of culture, but no single definition that all social scientists would heartily accept. Culture can be defined as the way of life of a social group; the total human-made environment (Theodorson & Theodorson, 1969). Although culture is often defined in a way that includes all the material and nonmaterial aspects of group life, most social scientists today emphasize the intangible, symbolic, and ideational aspect of culture.

It is the values, symbols, interpretations, and perspectives that distinguish one people from another in modernized societies, and not artifacts, material objects, and other tangible aspects of human societies. Values, norms, and perspectives distinguish ethnic groups such as Native Americans, African Americans, and Jewish Americans rather than the foods they eat or the clothes they wear. The essence of an ethnic culture in a modernized society such as the United States is its unique values, beliefs, symbols, and perspectives. Consequently, when a teacher teaches about groups such as Native Americans and Mexican Americans by having the students build teepees or eat tacos, they have missed the essence of the cultures of these groups and given the students misleading and distorted conceptions of their cultures.

Cultures are dynamic, complex, and changing. When teaching about the cultures of groups such as African Americans, Jewish Americans, and Japanese Americans, the teacher should be careful to help students to understand how such factors as time of immigration, social class, region, religion, gender, exceptionality, and education influence the behaviors and values of both individuals and subgroups within an ethnic group. An East Coast, upper middle-class, college-educated Chicana (Mexican American female) whose family has been in the United States since the turn of the century will differ in significant ways from a male Mexican migrant worker in California who has lived in the United States less than two decades.

Teachers should help students to understand the complex nature of ethnic groups in order to prevent them from developing new stereotypes when ethnic groups are studied in school. Any discussion of the modal characteristics of an ethnic group must be mediated by a consideration of how individual members of the group may differ from the group norms and characteristics in significant ways.

Macrocultures and Microcultures

The concept of culture as formulated by most social scientists does not deal with variations within the national culture or the smaller cultures within it. However, when dealing with multicultural education, it is necessary to describe variations within the national culture because multicultural education focuses on equal educational opportunities for different groups within the national culture. Two related concepts can help us deal with cultural variation within the national culture. We can call the national or shared culture of the nation-state or society the big culture, or *macroculture*. The smaller cultures that constitute it can be called *microcultures*.

Every nation-state has overarching values, symbols, and ideations that are to some degree shared by all microcultures. Various microcultural groups within the nation, however, may mediate, interpret, reinterpret, perceive, and experience these overarching national values and ideals differently.

The national, overarching ideals, symbols, and values can be described for various nation-states. Myrdal, the Swedish economist, identifies values such as justice, equality, and human dignity as overarching values in the United States (Myrdal, 1944). He calls these the American Creed values. Myrdal also describes the "American Dilemma" as an integral part of U.S. society. This dilemma results from the fact that even though most U.S. citizens internalize American Creed values, such as justice and human dignity, they often violate them in their daily behavior. Myrdal concludes that a tremendous gap exists between American democratic ideals and American realities, such as racism and sexism. Other U.S. overarching values include the Protestant work ethic, individualism as opposed to group orientation, distance, and materialism and material progress.

HISTORICAL AND CULTURAL KNOWLEDGE OF ETHNIC GROUPS

Teachers need a sound knowledge base about the history and culture of ethnic groups in order to successfully integrate ethnic content into the school curriculum (Acuña, 1988; Banks, 1991; Franklin & Moss, 1988; Rodriguez, 1989; Takaki, 1989). However, factual knowledge about ethnic groups is necessary but not sufficient. This knowledge needs to be organized and taught with key concepts (e.g., powerful ideas), themes, and issues in the experiences of ethnic and cultural groups. The experiences of ethnic groups in the United States can be viewed and compared by using several key, powerful concepts and ideas. I will describe 11 such concepts and discuss how they can be used to view and study the experiences of selected ethnic groups. These 11 key concepts are summarized in Table 4–1. Chapter 5 contains teaching units that describe how to teach two of these concepts: *knowledge construction* and *revolution*.

Key Concepts for Studying the Experiences of Ethnic and Cultural Groups

1. *Origins and Immigration.* When studying about an ethnic group in the United States, it is important to examine its origins and immigration

TABLE 4–1   Key Concepts to Guide the Study of Ethnic and Cultural Groups

1. Origins and immigration
2. Shared culture, values, and symbols
3. Ethnic identity and sense of peoplehood
4. Perspectives, world views, and frames of reference
5. Ethnic institutions and self-determination
6. Demographic, social, political, and economic status
7. Prejudice, discrimination, and racism
8. Intraethnic diversity
9. Assimilation and acculturation
10. Revolution
11. Knowledge construction

patterns. Most groups in the United States came from other lands. However, archeologists believe the Native Americans entered North America by crossing the Bering Strait between 45,000 and 40,000 years ago (Snipp, 1989). However, when studying about the origins of the first Americans, it is important to point out to students that many Native Americans believe that they were created in this land by the Great Sprit (Neihardt, 1972). Both perspectives on the origins of Native Americans should be presented and respected in the multicultural classroom.

The ancestors of the Mexican Americans are also natives to the Americas. A new people were created when the Spanish conquistadors and the Indians of the Americas produced children who were called *mestizos*. When the United States acquired about one-third of Mexico's territory at the end of the United States-Mexican War in 1848, about 80,000 Mexicans became U.S. citizens (Acuña, 1988). Today, about half of the growth in the Mexican population results from immigration; the other half is from new births (U.S. Bureau of the Census, 1992).

2. *Shared Culture, Values, and Symbols.* Most ethnic groups in the United States, especially ethnic minority groups, have unique cultures and values that resulted from an interaction of their original culture with the host culture in the United States, from ethnic institutions created partly as a response to discrimination, and from their social-class status. These cultures are still in the process of formation and change. They cannot and should not be viewed as static.

Examples of unique values and cultures of ethnic groups include the strong family orientation of Italian Americans (Tomasi, 1985), the strong identity with their tribe and kinship group among Native Americans (Allen, 1986), and the group orientation of African Americans (White & Parham, 1990). Black English, a dialect of English spoken by many

African Americans, is also an example of an ethnic cultural characteristic (Heath, 1983; Kochman, 1981).

3. *Ethnic Identity and Sense of Peoplehood.* A shared sense of peoplehood and ethnic identity is one of the most important characteristics of ethnic groups in the United States (Gordon, 1964). This shared sense of identity results from a common history and current experiences. Ethnic groups tend to view themselves and to be viewed by others as separate and apart from other groups in society. In the case of ethnic groups of color, such as African Americans and Mexican Americans, their shared sense of identity and peoplehood is reinforced by the racism and discrimination they experience. The shared sense of identity of an ethnic group can and often does extend beyond national boundaries. Most Jews in New York and London share feelings about the Holocaust. Most African Americans strongly identify with the struggle of the Blacks in South Africa.

4. *Perspectives, World Views, and Frames of Reference.* Members of the same ethnic group often view reality in a similar way and differently from other groups within a society. This results largely from their shared sense of peoplehood and identity described above. Most Hispanics in the United States tend to have positive views toward bilingual education and believe that their children should be able to speak both Spanish and English (Crawford, 1989).

5. *Ethnic Institutions and Self-Determination.* Many ethnic institutions were formed by groups in the United States in response to discrimination and segregation, such as African American churches, schools, colleges, and insurance companies, and Japanese and Jewish social organizations. Many of these institutions continue to exist today because they help ethnic groups to satisfy unique social, cultural, and educational needs. Other ethnic institutions, such as the National Association for the Advancement of Colored People, the Anti-Defamation League of B'nai B'rith, the League of United Latin-American Citizens, and the Japanese American Citizenship League, were formed to work for the civil rights of specific ethnic groups and to fight discrimination.

6. *Demographic, Social, Political, and Economic Status.* When acquiring knowledge about ethnic groups in the United States, their current demographic, social, political, and economic status needs to be determined. The economic profile of Filipino Americans was one of the lowest in the United States in the 1960s. However, they now have a high economic status, primarily because of the large number of professional workers that immigrated to the United States from the Philippines during the

1970s and 1980s (Daniels, 1988; Takaki, 1989). The number of Asians and Pacific Islanders in the United States increased from 3.5 million in 1980 to 7.3 million in 1990—a 107.8 percent increase—compared to a 53 percent increase for Hispanics, a 13.2 percent increase for African Americans, a 6 percent increase for Whites, and a 9.8 percent increase for the total U.S. population. In 1990, the Asian and Pacific Islander population of the United States was 7,274,000. In 1990, the U.S. total population reached a record 248,710,000 (U.S. Bureau of the Census, 1992).

The economic and educational status of an ethnic group can change. There was significant improvement in the economic and educational status of African Americans and Hispanics during the 1960s and 1970s. However, during the 1980s these groups lost ground in both economic and educational status. Census figures released in 1988 indicate that during the 1980s, the percentage of Whites living below the poverty level decreased, whereas the percentage of African Americans and Hispanics living below the poverty increased. In 1990, 8.1 percent of Whites; 25 percent of Hispanics; 29.3 percent of African Americans, and 10.7 percent of all races lived below the poverty level (U.S. Bureau of the Census, 1992).

7. *Prejudice, Discrimination, and Racism.* Whenever groups with different racial, ethnic, and cultural characteristics interact, ethnocentrism, discrimination, and racism develop (van den Berghe, 1978). When discrimination based on race becomes institutionalized within a society and the dominant group has the power to implement its racial ideology within these institutions, institutional racism exists. Groups such as African Americans, Native Americans, Asian Americans, and Hispanics have been historically and are today victims of institutional racism in the United States. However, racism in the United States today is much more subtle and less blatant than it was prior to the Civil Rights Movement of the 1960s and 1970s. Some of the most blatant forms were eradicated during that period, largely in response to the Civil Rights Movement.

Prejudice, discrimination, and *racism* are important concepts for understanding the experiences of ethnic groups in the past, present, and future, not only in the United States but in nations throughout the world.

8. *Intraethnic Diversity.* Even though ethnic groups share a culture, values, a sense of identity, and a common history, there are tremendous differences within ethnic groups. These important differences must always be kept in mind when we study an ethnic group. If not, we may create new stereotypes and misconceptions. These differences result from such factors as region (e.g., whether rural or urban), social class, religion, age, gender, and political affiliation. While it is important to recognize that ethnic groups share many important characteristics, keep in mind that we are describing *groups,* not *individuals.* An individual may embrace all or hardly any of the dominant characteristics of his or her ethnic group. This individual may also have a strong or a weak identity with his or her ethnic group.

9. *Assimilation and Acculturation.* When an ethnic or cultural group assimilates, it gives up its characteristics and adopts those of another group (Gordon, 1964). Acculturation describes the process that occurs when the characteristics of a group are changed because of interaction with another cultural or ethnic group. When acculturation occurs, the interacting groups exchange cultural characteristics; thus, both are changed in the process.

Assimilation and acculturation are important for understanding the experiences of ethnic groups in the United States and the world. In most societies, the dominant ethnic or cultural group expects other groups to adopt its language, culture, values, and behavior. Cultural conflict usually develops within modernized societies when ethnic minority groups hold on to many of their important cultural characteristics or when they are denied full participation in the dominant society after they have culturally assimilated to a large degree. The dominant cultural group within a society, such as the Anglo-Saxon Protestants in the United States, often adopt cultural traits from ethnic minority groups, such as African Americans and Indians, without acknowledging them or giving them appropriate recognition. The contributions that African Americans and Native Americans have made to American literature, government, and music are rarely acknowledged fully (Weatherford, 1992).

10. *Revolution.* A political revolution takes place when a fundamental change takes place in the leadership of a society (Theodorson & Theodorson, 1969), usually through violent upheaval and armed conflict. Other basic changes within a society, which often take place over a long period of time, are also described as revolutions, such as the industrial and agricultural revolutions. These revolutions are gradual transformations of a society rather than sudden changes. Revolution is an important concept for understanding the history of most ethnic groups in the United States because of the influence of revolutions on their past. Revolution is also an important concept in the history of ethnic groups in the United States because the ideas related to it—such as oppression, alienation, and hope for change—have been decisive in the history of U.S. ethnic groups.

In 1680, an important American revolution occurred when the Pueblo Indians in New Spain (New Mexico) rebelled against their Spanish conquerors. The revolution was not successful in the long run because the Pueblos were eventually reconquered by the Spaniards with deadly vengeance.

Students need to view the revolution in the British colonies from a multicultural perspective to fully understand it because it had different meanings for different groups such as the Anglo Loyalists, the Anglo Revolutionaries, the various Native American groups, and the African Americans. Some ethnic groups in the United States fled their native lands in search of freedom in the United States after revolutions occurred there. When Castro took control of Cuba in 1959, thousands of Cubans sought refuge in the United States. The Cuban refugees who came to the United States during and in the years following the Castro revolution constitute the bedrock of today's Cuban American population.

11. *Knowledge Construction.* When studying the history and contemporary experiences of ethnic and cultural groups in the United States, it is important for students to understand how knowledge and interpretations are constructed. They also need to understand how cultural experiences, biases, and values influence the knowledge construction process (Harding, 1991). A transformative, multicultural curriculum also helps students to construct their own interpretations. The constructivist approach to teaching and learning is a key component of the transformative, multicultural curriculum.

When teachers engage students in knowledge construction, the students are given opportunities to participate in building knowledge and to construct their own interpretations of historical, social, and current events. The knowledge construction approach to teaching is constructivist in orientation and is influenced by the work of the Russian psychologist L. S. Vygotsky (Cole, John-Steiner, Scribner, & Souberman, 1978; Wertsch, 1985).

Knowledge construction is influenced significantly by the group experience of the knower. The knowledge constructed within a group is incorporated into the group's legends, myths, heroes, and heroines, and reflects the group's values and beliefs. For example, the Battle of Little Big Horn can be viewed as a noble defense of one's homeland (the Native American version) or as a vicious massacre of soldiers who were protecting Anglo American pioneers (the dominant Anglo American view at the time) (Garcia, 1993).

Knowledge construction is a powerful idea in multicultural education because it can be taught in all disciplines and content areas. It can be used to help students understand the values and assumptions that underlie the base-ten number system in mathematics, the scientific method in the natural and biological sciences, and literary interpretations in the language arts and humanities. Knowledge construction is also a powerful idea that can guide the development of activities and teaching strategies that will enable students to build their own interpretations of the past, present, and future.

5

TEACHING WITH POWERFUL IDEAS

Can you list all of the major battles that occurred during the American Revolution or name each of the 50 state capitals? If you are like most people, you can't. Research indicates that people forget a very large percentage of the facts they learn (Klausmeier & Goodwin, 1971). What most people remember about the American Revolution is not all of the major battles that occurred but the major reasons why the Revolution took place and what happened when it ended.

Most people can remember that many state capitals are located in smaller cities rather than in the largest city within a state. Albany, rather than New York City, is the capital of New York; Springfield is the capital of Illinois, not Chicago; Olympia is the capital of Washington, not Seattle.

People tend to remember big, powerful ideas rather than factual details. Big ideas are not only remembered longer but they help people to gain a better understanding of events and phenomena, to categorize and classify observations, and to transfer knowledge from one situation to another.

THE CONCEPTUAL APPROACH

The big, powerful ideas that people tend to remember and that facilitate understanding and transfer of knowledge are called *concepts* and *gener-*

alizations (Banks with Clegg, 1990). In the conceptual approach to teaching, the curriculum as well as units and lessons are organized around key concepts and generalizations from the various disciplines and subject areas. These powerful ideas help students to organize and synthesize large amounts of data and information (Taba et al., 1971).

THE CATEGORIES OF KNOWLEDGE

In order to develop and teach a multicultural curriculum that focuses on powerful concepts and ideas, you need to understand the knowledge categories and their interrelationships: facts, concepts and generalizations (Banks, 1991a). *Facts* are low-level, specific empirical statements. *Concepts* are words or phrases that enable people to categorize or classify a large class of observations and thus to reduce the complexity of their world. *Generalizations* are tested or verified statements that contain two or more concepts and state how they are related. Table 5–1 contains examples of these knowledge categories.

The treatment of concepts and generalizations is succinct in this book because of its brevity. Readers who would like a more detailed discussion of the knowledge categories as well as historical overviews of the major U.S. ethnic groups should see *Teaching Strategies for Ethnic Studies* (Banks, 1991a).

TABLE 5–1   The Categories of Knowledge

Concept: *Social Protest*

Fact: On February 1, 1960, the sit-in movement designed to end racially segregated accommodation facilities began when a group of African American students sat down at a lunch counter reserved for Whites at a Woolworth's store in Greensboro, North Carolina.

Lower-Level Generalization: The sit-in movement, boycotts, and the Black Power movement were part of a larger movement in the 1960s and 1970s whose goal was to end institutionalized racism and discrimination.

Intermediate-Level Generalization: The Civil Rights Movement in the United States spread as women, people with disabilities, and gays and lesbians started organized movements to end discrimination against their respective groups.

High-Level/Universal Generalization: When a group perceives itself as oppressed and believes that there is a possibility for a change and reform, it will initiate organized protest and resistance.

A CONCEPTUAL MULTICULTURAL CURRICULUM

To build a conceptual, multicultural curriculum, it is necessary to choose higher-level, powerful concepts like *culture, power, socialization, protest,* and *values* as organizing concepts. One of the best conceptual curriculums was developed by Hilda Taba and her colleagues (Taba et al., 1971). It is a social studies curriculum designed for grades 1 through 8. *The Taba Social Studies Curriculum* is organized around these powerful, organizing concepts:

Causality	Modification
Conflict	Power
Cooperation	Societal control
Cultural change	Tradition
Differences	Values
Interdependence	

Powerful, organizing concepts for an interdisciplinary multicultural curriculum may be discipline specific, such as *culture* from anthropology and *socialization* from sociology. They may also be interdisciplinary, such as *modification* and *causality*, used in the *Taba Social Studies Curriculum.*

How to Develop a Multicultural Conceptual Curriculum

   1. *Identify key concepts, such as ethnic diversity, immigration, and assimilation, around which you will organize your curriculum.*   When choosing concepts around which to organize your curriculum, lessons, or units, keep these criteria in mind:

a. The concepts should be powerful ones that can be used to organize a large quantity and scope of data and information.
b. The concepts should be ones that can be used to organize and classify information from a range of disciplines and subject areas, such as the social sciences, literature and the language arts, and, when possible, the physical, natural, and biological sciences. *Ethnic diversity* (discussed later) is such a concept.
c. Consider the developmental level of your students, in terms of their chronological age, cognitive development, moral development, and their prior experiences with ethnic and cultural content. *Prejudice* and *discrimination* are much more appropriate concepts to teach to young children than racism.

Taba and her colleagues (1971, p. 28) recommend that the first four questions guide the selection of key concepts for a conceptual curriculum. I added the fifth criteria question.

a. *Validity:* Do they adequately represent concepts of the disciplines from which they are drawn?
b. *Significance:* Can they explain important segments of the world today, and are they descriptive of important aspects of human behavior?
c. *Durability:* Are they of lasting importance?
d. *Balance:* Do they permit development of student thinking in both scope and depth?
e. *Ethnic and cultural relevance:* Do they help students to better understand the experiences of ethnic groups in the United States and the world?

2. *Identify key or universal generalizations related to each of the key concepts chosen.*

3. *Identify an intermediate-level generalization for each of the key concepts.*

4. *Identify a lower-level generalization related to the key generalization for each of the subject areas in which the key concept will be taught.* The multicultural conceptual curriculum is interdisciplinary. Concepts are selected that can be used to incorporate information and data from several disciplines. In the example in Table 5–2, *ethnic diversity* is taught in each subject area. In actual practice, the concepts are likely to be taught in only two or three subject areas at the same time. Interdisciplinary teaching often requires team planning and teaching at the middle school level and beyond. Table 5–2 shows ethnic diversity being taught in each subject area to illustrate the powerful potential of the conceptual approach to teaching.

5. *Formulate teaching strategies and activities to teach the concepts and generalizations.* Teaching strategies for these two concepts are described in the second part of this chapter: (1) *the construction of historical knowledge* and (2) *revolutions.*

THE SPIRAL DEVELOPMENT OF CONCEPTS AND GENERALIZATIONS

In a conceptual, multicultural curriculum, the key concepts and generalizations identified are taught and developed at an increasing degree of complexity and depth throughout the grades. New content samples are

TABLE 5–2 Teaching Ethnic Diversity in All Subject Areas

Key Concept: *Ethnic Diversity*

Key or Organizing Generalization: Most societies are characterized by ethnic diversity.

Intermediate-Level Generalization: Ethnic diversity is an important characteristic of the United States.

Lower-Level Generalizations:
Social Studies
The new wave of immigration to the United States since the 1960s has increased ethnic diversity within it.

Language Arts
Ethnic diversity is reflected in the variety of language and communication patterns in the United States.

Music
Ethnic diversity in the United States is reflected in its folk, gospel, and popular music.

Drama
The plays written by U.S. authors of varying ethnic backgrounds have enriched the national culture.

Physical and Movement Education
Dance and other forms of expressive movements in the United States reflect the nation's ethnic diversity.

Art
The visual arts in the United States reflect the nation's rich ethnic makeup.

Home Economics and Family Living
Ethnic diversity in the United States is reflected in the nation's foods and family life-styles.

Science
The diverse physical characteristics of the people in the United States reinforce ethnic diversity.

Mathematics
Mathematical notations and systems in the United States reflect the contributions of many different ethnic, racial, and cultural groups. This is rarely recognized.

---

used at each subsequent grade level to help the students learn the concepts and generalizations at an increasing degree of depth and complexity. Figure 5–1 illustrates how *social protest,* a concept, is introduced in fifth grade and is taught with increasing depth and complexity through grade 12.

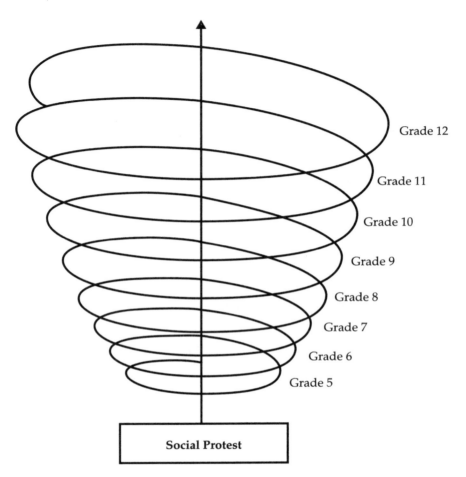

Grade 12

Grade 11

Grade 10

Grade 9

Grade 8

Grade 7

Grade 6

Grade 5

Social Protest

FIGURE 5–1   **Social Protest Is Taught at Grades 5 Through 12 at an Increasing Degree of Depth and Complexity**

SOCIAL SCIENCE AND VALUE INQUIRY SKILLS

It is very important for students to master facts, concepts, and generalizations, but it is just as important, if not more so, for them to gain proficiency in the processes involved in gathering and evaluating knowledge, identifying the biases and assumptions that underlie knowledge claims, and constructing knowledge themselves. An important goal of the multicultural curriculum is to help students develop proficiency in inquiry and thinking skills such as stating research questions and problems, hypothesizing, conceptualizing, collecting and analyzing data, and deriving generalizations and conclusions. The steps of social science inquiry are described by Banks (with Clegg, 1990).

Although knowledge and skills goals are very important, it is essential that a multicultural curriculum help students develop the skills needed to reflect on their moral choices and to make thoughtful decisions. I have developed a value inquiry model (described later) that can be used to help students develop value inquiry skills. Students should be provided with opportunities to develop democratic values and to act on their moral decisions. Values education is especially important in multicultural education because prejudice and discrimination, which multicultural education tries to reduce, are heavily value laden. The moral dimension of multicultural education is discussed in the last part of this chapter.

EXAMPLES OF LESSONS ORGANIZED WITH POWERFUL CONCEPTS

Teaching about Historical Bias and Knowledge Construction

The knowledge construction component of multicultural education helps students understand how knowledge is constructed and how it is influential by the biases, experiences, and perceptions of historians and other researchers (Banks, 1993a; Code, 1991; Collins, 1990; Harding, 1991). It also helps students to construct their own versions of the past, present, and future. In knowledge construction lessons and units, students are active participants in building knowledge rather than passive consumers of the knowledge constructed by others. What follows is a unit written by the author (Banks with Sebesta, 1982) that is designed to teach junior high students how knowledge is constructed in history and about how historical interpretations are derived.

Columbus and the Arawaks

During the fifteenth century, Europeans wanted to find an easy way to reach Asia. They wanted to trade with Asian merchants. Many Europeans knew that the world is round. They believed they could reach Asia by sailing west. Christopher Columbus, an Italian sailor and explorer, was one who wanted to prove that it could be done. For many years, he tried to find money to sail west to reach Asia, also called the East Indies. Finally, King Ferdinand and Queen Isabella of Spain agreed to support his voyage. On August 3, 1492, Columbus sailed from Palos, Spain. His three small ships were called the *Pinta,* the *Nina,* and the *Santa Maria.* On October 12, 1492, Columbus and his crew landed on San Salvador in the Bahamas Islands. The Bahamas Islands are located in what are now called the West Indies. We use that name because of the mistake Columbus made. He was sure he had landed near India. Even after other European explorers visited America, people still believed that America was part of the East Indies. This is why the Europeans called the Native Americans "Indians."

Columbus Writes about the Arawaks

In a letter that Columbus wrote in 1493, he tells of meeting with the people he called Indians (Muzzey, 1915, p. 8).

> *They believed very firmly that I, with these ships and crews, came from the sky.... Wherever I arrived they went running from house to house and to the neighboring villages, with loud cries of "Come! Come to see the people from Heaven!"*

Columbus Describes the Arawaks at San Salvador

Columbus kept a diary of his first voyage across the ocean. Here is what he wrote about the Arawaks when he first met them on San Salvador (Jane, 1989, pp. 23–24). Does he report facts only? Does he mix his own opinion with the facts?

> *I, ... in order that they might feel great amity towards us, because I knew that they were a people to be delivered and converted to our holy faith rather by love than by force, gave to some among them some red caps and some glass beads, which they hung round their necks, and many other things of little value. At this they were greatly pleased and became so entirely our friends that it was a wonder to see. Afterwards they came swimming to the ships' boats, where we were, and brought us parrots and cotton thread in balls, and spears and many other things, and we exchanged for them other things, such as small glass beads and hawks' bells, which we gave to them. In fact, they took all and gave all, such as they had, with good will, but it seemed to me that they were a people very deficient in everything. They all go naked as their mothers bore them, and the women also, although I saw only one very young girl. And all those whom I did see were youths, so that I did not see one who was over thirty years of age;*

they were very well built, with very handsome bodies and very good faces. Their hair is coarse almost like the hairs of a horse's tail and short; they wear their hair down over their eyebrows, except for a few strands behind, which they wear long and never cut. Some of them are painted black, and they are the colour of the people of the Canaries, neither black nor white, and some of them are painted white and some red and some in any colour that they find. Some of them paint their faces, some their whole bodies, some only the eyes, and some only the nose. They do not bear arms or know them, for I showed to them swords and they took them by the blade and cut themselves through ignorance. They have no iron. Their spears are certain reeds, without iron, and some of these have a fish tooth at the end, while others are pointed in various ways. They are all generally fairly tall, good looking and well proportioned. I saw some who bore marks of wounds on their bodies, and I made signs to them to ask how this came about, and they indicated to me that people came from other islands, which are near, and wished to capture them, and they defended themselves. And I believed and still believe that they come here from the mainland to take them for slaves. They should be good servants and of quick intelligence, since I see that they very soon say all that is said to them, and I believe that they would easily be made Christians, for it appeared to me that they had no creed. Our Lord willing, at the time of my departure I will bring back six of them to Your Highnesses, that they may learn to talk. I saw no beast of any kind in this island, except parrots.

The Second Voyage of Columbus

Columbus sailed back to Spain on January 16, 1493. Later that same year, he set off on his second voyage. This time he explored other islands, including those now called Puerto, the Virgin Islands, and Jamaica.

On his first trip, Columbus had established a trading post on the island of Hispaniola, where Haiti and the Dominican Republic are now located. When he returned to Hispaniola, he found that his trading post had been destroyed. This is what had happened. The men Columbus had left in charge of the trading post had been cruel to the Arawaks. The Arawaks became angry. One of them was a man named Caonabo (ka o na' bo). He led a group of Arawaks who killed the Spaniards and then destroyed the trading post. When Columbus discovered what had happened, he and his men attacked the Arawaks and defeated them. Caonabo was sent to Spain for punishment.

Columbus's Demands for Gold

Columbus set up a new trading post right away. It was very important for him to find gold in America and send it back to Spain. He had to please the Spanish king and queen.

Columbus did not really have any way of knowing how much gold there was in Hispaniola. In order to get as much gold as possible, he devised a plan. He told the Arawaks in the gold-producing region that they must honor the Spanish king. Every three months, all of the Arawaks fourteen years old or older had to give Columbus a small amount of gold dust. Each Arawak who gave the gold wore a piece of brass or copper around his or her neck to prove that the payment had been made. Any Arawak found without the neck ornament was punished. There was not enough gold in Hispaniola to satisfy Columbus. The Arawaks could not meet his demand for gold. Some tried to escape to the mountains. Some became ill and died. Some starved. Some who could not pay the gold were tortured and killed. Others were forced to work the land or were sent in slavery to Spain.

Ferdinand, Son of Columbus

Columbus had a son named Ferdinand who went with him on his fourth trip to America in 1502. At that time, Ferdinand was just thirteen years old. When he was grown, Ferdinand wrote about his father in a book called *The Life of the Admiral Christopher Columbus* (Keen, 1959, p. 150). Here is what Ferdinand said about the way his father treated the Arawaks.

> *After the capture of Caonabo the island was so peaceful that a Christian could safely go wherever he pleased, and the Indians themselves offered to carry him piggyback, as they do nowadays at the post stages. Columbus credits this peace to the favor of God and the good fortune of the Catholic monarchs [kings], else it would have been impossible for 200 poorly armed men, half of them sick, to defeat a mass of Indians. But the Lord wished to punish the Indians, and so brought them a shortage of food and such a variety of diseases that he reduced their number by two-thirds, that it might be clear that such wonderful conquests came from His supreme hand and not from our strength or wit or the cowardice of the Indians.*

The Arawaks

What was life really like for the Arawaks that Ferdinand believed were "punished" by God? Their culture came to an end a century after the Spaniards came to their home in the Caribbean Islands. But archaeologists, using artifacts, are able to piece together the story of the Arawaks.

An archaeologist named Fred Olsen (1974) studied Arawak artifacts. From what he learned from these artifacts, he wrote a description of what an Arawak community was probably like. He tried to tell what life was like for the Arawaks in 1490, which was two years before Columbus came to San Salvador in the Bahamas Islands. Here is Fred Olsen's description of what might have happened during one day in an Arawak village (Olsen, pp. 217–219, ff. 119–120).

A group of men is making a canoe, which they use when they catch fish. They need the fish because it is the main source of protein in the Arawak diet. A tree, which is about four inches [ten centimeters] round and twenty feet [six meters] long, has already been felled [cut down] and is on the ground. On top of the trunk the men have started a series of small fires, about a foot [thirty centimeters] apart. The fires have been burning for two or three hours. Now the charcoal is being scooped out with shell-like stone axes. The ridges of burned wood remaining between the fire pits are being split off by stone tools with wooden handles. The burned wood is brittle. The burning, chipping, and scooping out will continue until a great deal of wood is removed from the center of the log. Then the walls will be stretched enough to allow the seats to be put in. The leader of the group knows this large fishing canoe will take at least six moons [months] to finish before it can be paddled down the river to the sea.

Several men, who have just spent a few days at the coast, are bringing back a canoe-load of turtles from the ocean. At the end of the village, pottery is being made by the women . . . and the pots lying on the live coals are almost fully fired [baked]. A few more branches are put on the fire to finish baking the pots. Nearby, two women are pressing, folding, and stretching reddish clay. The best clay is found not far from the river. Small amounts of water and sand are being added until the clay has the right form. The women roll long rods of the clay, about the thickness of a finger. They coil these rods layer by layer, higher and higher until the basic shape of their pot is formed. Two types of pottery are being made today: large cooking vessels and griddles to cook cassava bread. The cooking pots are sixteen inches [forty centime-

ters] round and ten inches [twenty-five centimeters] deep and have
a wide mouth.

   In one hut lies a man who has been ill for several days. The
shaman [priest-doctor] has been called. He is now blowing smoke
over the sick man, directing it at the point of pain. The sick man
is very familiar with the tobacco which the shaman smokes before
he goes into a state of trance [deep sleep]. The use of tobacco
during his treatment is considered very important in the curing of
his illness. The shaman is calling the good spirits to come and
help him.

   Just beyond the trees surrounding the villages are the fields
where cassava is grown. About 80 percent of the Arawaks' daily
food is made up of cassava bread. Some of the fields are almost
cleared of fallen trees and stumps. These are the fields that have
been farmed the longest. They lie near the stream and are kept
fertile when the rains from the surrounding hills flood the area
and bring new silt to the soil. The women are gathering their day's
supply of cassava. They bend to feel the size of the tubers [the
thick parts of underground stems] at the base of the cassava stem.
When these are large enough, the plant is pulled up and the tubers
are loaded into a wicker pack and carried back to the hut.

   More fields are needed as families grow in size, and as the soil
becomes less fertile. This is man's work. A dozen men are building
fires around the base of the trees to eat away the wood until the
tree falls. This new field is now a tangle of trees that have fallen
in all directions. But before the rain comes, the slashed area will
be burned.

When Columbus first came to the Caribbean Islands in 1492,
there were about three hundred thousand Arawaks living there. One
hundred years later, almost none remained. Forced labor and dis-
eases destroyed most of the Arawaks.

The Last Journeys of Columbus

Columbus made his two final journeys in 1498 and 1502. During
these voyages, he sailed along the coast of Central America and
South America. Columbus died in 1506, still thinking he had
reached the Indies. He never knew that he had explored the conti-
nent of America.

   In this unit, you have read about the landing of Columbus in
America, and the effect he and other Spaniards had on the Arawaks.
In the next chapter, you will read about other European explorers
who came to America.

What Do You Think?

1. Columbus wrote in his diary that he thought the Indians had no religious beliefs. You read about Arawak life in the report by Fred Olsen. Do you think Columbus was correct? Why?
2. Accounts written by people who took part in or witnessed (saw) an historical event are called primary sources. Can historians believe everything they read in a primary source? Explain.

Things to Do

1. Be an Arawak in 1492. Working with three other classmates, write a response to Columbus's account on pages 66–67.
2. Working in a group with three other students, and using the documents in this unit as your source, write your own account of the Columbus-Arawak encounter. Then answer these questions:

    a. In what ways is your account limited?
    b. What can you do that would make your account less limited?
    c. Are historical accounts always limited no matter how many documents, artifacts, and resources the historian has? Why or why not?
    d. What conclusions can you make about the writing of historical accounts based on this activity?

3. Carl Becker, the famous historian, said that every person was his or her own historian. What did he mean? To what extent is his statement accurate?

TEACHING ABOUT REVOLUTIONS USING SOCIAL SCIENCE INQUIRY

Social Science Inquiry

In the unit on *revolutions* described below, Ms. Garcia, a senior high school social studies teacher, uses the inquiry model developed by Banks (Banks with Clegg, 1990)—illustrated in Figure 5–2—to teach a powerful concept: *revolution*. She uses three American revolutions as content samples: (1) the Pueblo Revolution in 1680, in which the Pueblo tribes of New Mexico revolted against the Spanish; (2) the revolution in the British Colonies (1776); and (3) the Mexican Revolution of 1810.

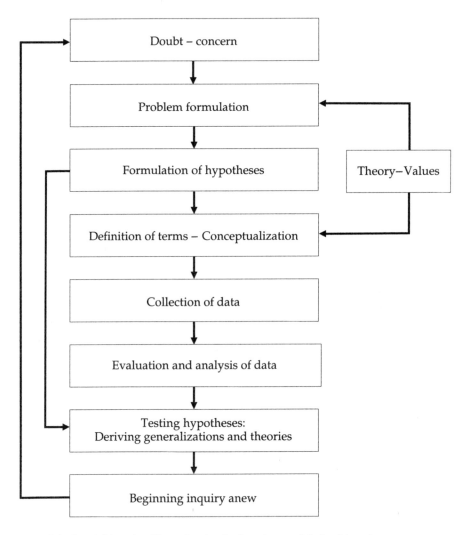

A model of social inquiry. Note that in the inquiry model, doubt and concern cause the inquirer to formulate a problem. The problem that he or she fomulates does not emanate from a vacuum, but is shaped by his or her theoretical and value orientation. Like the social scientist, the student will need to draw on *knowlede* to be able to ask intelligent and fruitful questions. In social science inquiry, *theory* is the main source of fruitful questions. While these are the basic steps of social inquiry, they do not necessarily occur in the order illustrated above. This figure indicates that generalizations in social science are continually tested and are never regarded as absolute. Thus, social inquiry is cyclic rather than linear and fixed.

FIGURE 5–2   A Model of Social Inquiry

Source: Teaching Strategies for the Social Studies: Inquiry, Valuing, and Decision-Making, 4th edition, by James A. Banks, with Ambrose A. Clegg, Jr. Copyright © 1990 by Longman Publishing Group. Used with permission.

Creating Doubt and Concern: Motivating the Students

Ms. Garcia starts the unit by having the class play the simulation game, *Star Power* (Shirts, 1969). In this game, after a round of trading chips, the players are divided into three groups according to the number of points they have: the *squares* (with the most points), the *circles* (with the least points), and the *triangles* (those in between). Ms. Garcia then distributes the chips in such a way, without the players knowing it, that will keep the squares ahead of the other two groups.

A highly stratified society is created with little opportunity for mobility. When they are in a clearly dominant position, Ms. Garcia gives the squares the power to make the rules of the game. They make rules that help to keep themselves in power. The circles and the triangles become deeply angry and frustrated and call the rules dictatorial and fascist. The frustrations become so high that the game ends in a revolt against the rules and the squares.

Formulating Questions and Hypotheses

Ms. Garcia uses the simulation game as a vehicle to start the unit on revolutions and to get the students to formulate questions related to the rise of pre-revolutionary conditions in a society. She asks the students:

1. Why did the circles and the triangles become so angry and frustrated?
2. Have you ever had a real-life experience in which you felt this way? If so, what was it? Why did you feel that way? What did you do about it?
3. How did the simulation game end? Why did it end that way?
4. Can you think of examples of people and groups in history and in modern times who felt the way the triangles and circles felt at the end of the game?

Through questions and cues, Ms. Garcia gets the students to discuss these examples: (1) the Pilgrims in seventeenth-century England who were opposed to the Church of England; (2) the American colonists in the late 1700s who were angry with Britain about taxation without representation; (3) the Cherokee Indians in the Southeast in the 1830s who were forced to move from their homeland to Oklahoma; (4) the Jews in Germany in the 1940s who experienced discrimination and persecution; and (5) African Americans in the South during the 1950s and 1960s who experienced discrimination.

What kinds of conditions made these groups angry? (Ms. Garcia is trying to get the students to state hypotheses about conditions that can lead to anger and rebellion. The class keeps a list of its statements about the kinds of conditions that made these groups so angry.)

Ms. Garcia asks the students to list some things that individuals and groups might be able to do when they feel like the triangles and the circles, like the Jews in Germany in the 1940s, or the American colonists in 1776. The students state that these groups might: (1) let the authorities know how unhappy they are; (2) try to change the laws and rules; or (3) migrate to another place or nation.

Ms. Garcia then asks: What if none of these things are possible? What if none of them helps to improve the conditions of those who feel mistreated? Then what might they do? Through continual questioning, cues, and examples, Ms. Garcia helps the students to state that if all efforts fail to improve their conditions, then groups might try to overthrow the government if certain conditions prevail.

Ms. Garcia tells the class that, depending on many conditions within a society, a group that feels mistreated may do many different things, including start a protest movement, migrate, start riots, and, in particular cases, try to overthrow the government. She points out that in most of the examples the class discussed, the groups did not try to overthrow the government. She asks: What particular conditions do you think must exist before a group that is very angry tries to overthrow the government? (Ms. Garcia is trying to get the students to hypothesize about the causes of *revolutions*. The class keeps a list of the hypotheses it states.)

Ms. Garcia asks the students to give their ideas about what they think happens when the old government is overthrown and a new government is established. (She is trying to get them to state hypotheses about what happens when a revolution occurs and a new government is established.) The class keeps a record of its hypotheses.

Ms. Garcia helps the students to summarize the major questions they have raised and will study during the unit:

1. What kinds of things make groups very angry within a nation or society?
2. What kinds of things do groups do when they are very angry about the way in which the government and officials of a nation are treating them?
3. Under what conditions will groups try to overthrow the government when they feel angry and mistreated?
4. What happens when the government is overthrown?
5. Does the new government remove the conditions that cause the old government to be overthrown?

Defining Concepts
Ms. Garcia tells the class that it has discussed two major ideas that social scientists use specific concepts to describe. The powerlessness and frus-

tration that the triangles and circles felt at the end of the simulation is called *alienation* by sociologists. Alienated individuals and groups feel that they cannot control their destiny or have any significant influence on the important events within their society (Theodorson & Theodorson, 1969). She tells the students that when the government of a nation is suddenly overthrown and a new government is established, a *revolution* has taken place. She gives the students Crane Brinton's (1962, p. 4) definition of a revolution: "The drastic, sudden substitution of one group in charge of the running of a territorial political entity for another group."

Ms. Garcia tells the class that *revolution* is used in many different ways (she gives examples of it, meaning a complete change in something) but that it will be used to mean the sudden replacement of one government by another in this unit.

Collecting Data

Ms. Garcia decides to use a combination of lectures, class discussions, and small groups to present and gather data. Drawing on materials primarily from the French Revolution of 1789, Ms. Garcia presents several lectures in which she sketches some of the major reasons that revolutions develop, some of their major characteristics, and what often happens in the postrevolutionary period. Each of her lectures is followed by a discussion session in which she asks the students higher-level questions that help them to develop concepts and generalizations about the characteristics of a revolution and the conditions under which they occur.

Ms. Garcia divides the class into three groups to do independent research on three American revolutions: the *Pueblo Revolution in 1680;* the *Revolution in the English Colonies in 1776;* and the *Mexican Revolution in 1810.* The class develops the data retrieval chart in Table 5–3 to guide the research of each group.

Ms. Garcia also plans some total-class data-gathering activities in addition to her lectures. The students read Chapters 1, 2, and 9 in *The Anatomy of Revolution* by Crane Brinton (1962). In this book, Brinton derives generalizations about revolutions by analyzing four: the English (1649), the American (1776), the French (1789), and the Russian (1917). The students also read George Orwell's (1946) *Animal Farm,* a disguised political satire of the Russian revolution.

Evaluating Data and Deriving Generalizations

When the three research groups collect their data, they analyze it, making sure that they answer all of the questions in Table 5–3. Each of the three groups presents its findings to the class in a different format. The group that studies the Pueblo Revolution presents its findings to the

TABLE 5–3   Data Retrieval Chart on Revolutions

Questions	Pueblo Revolution 1680	Revolution in the English Colonies 1776	Mexican Revolution 1810
Who were the people or groups in power?			
What people or groups wanted power?			
What were the major causes of the revolution?			
What incident(s) triggered the revolution?			
What was gained or lost and by whom?			
What happened immediately afterward?			
What happened in the long run?			

class in the form of a dramatization. A narrator describes the highlights of the revolution as the other students in the group act them out. This group describes how the Pueblo Revolution ultimately failed when the pueblos were reconquered by the Spanish.

> *Pope was dead. The Pueblo tribes had tired of fighting. They were ill and hungry. Vargas brought an army of less than a hundred soldiers to Santa Fe in 1692. Tall, sure of himself, and quiet in his manner, he took the town without fighting. Then he went from pueblo to pueblo convincing the Indians once again to accept Spanish rule, never firing a shot. In this way he "conquered" 73 pueblos for the Spanish.*

The English Colonies group prepares a striking mural that depicts the major events in that revolution. The students share this mural when making their class presentation. The Mexican Revolution group presents its findings to the class in a panel discussion.

During and after each group's presentation, using the data retrieval chart in Table 5–3, the class formulates generalizations about the three revolutions. The class discusses ways in which the three revolutions were alike and different. The Pueblo Revolution was the most different from the other two because it ultimately failed because the Pueblo tribes were eventually reconquered by the Spaniards. The students compare the generalizations they developed with those stated by Brinton in the last chapter of *The Anatomy of Revolution*. They also compare their findings with the view of a revolution presented in Orwell's *Animal Farm* and discuss the extent to which fiction can provide insights on social reality.

When the unit ends, Ms. Garcia has succeeded not only in helping the students to derive concepts and generalizations about revolutions but she has helped them gain a keen appreciation for the difficulties historians face in reconstructing historical events, establishing cause and effect, and formulating accurate generalizations.

VALUE INQUIRY IN THE MULTICULTURAL CURRICULUM

The multicultural curriculum should help students to identify, examine, and clarify their values; consider value alternatives, and make reflective value choices they can defend within a society in which human dignity is a shared value. You can use the value inquiry model I developed to help your students to identify and clarify their values and to make reflective moral choices (Banks with Clegg, 1990). The Banks' value inquiry model consists of these steps:

1. Defining and recognizing value problems
2. Describing value-relevant behavior
3. Naming values exemplified by the behavior
4. Determining conflicting values in behavior described
5. Hypothesizing about the possible consequences of the values analyzed
6. Naming alternative values to those exemplified by behavior observed
7. Hypothesizing about the possible consequences of values analyzed
8. Declaring value preferences: choosing
9. Stating reasons, sources, and possible consequences of value choice: justifying, hypothesizing, predicting

You can use a variety of materials and resources to simulate value inquiry and discussion of multicultural issues and topics, such as documents similar to the ones used in the preceding historical inquiry lesson, newspaper feature stories, textbook descriptions of issues and events, and open-ended stories like the one below. When using the open-ended story below, *Trying to Buy a Home in Lakewood Island* (Banks, 1991a, p. 220), you can use the value inquiry model above to develop questions like the ones that follow the story to simulate value discussion and decision-making:

Trying to Buy a Home in Lakewood Island

About a year ago, Joan and Henry Green, a young African American couple, moved from the West Coast to a large city in the Midwest. They moved because Henry finished his Ph.D. in chemistry and took a job at a big university in Midwestern City. Since they have been in Midwestern City, the Greens have rented an apartment in the central area of the city. However, they have decided that they want to buy a house. Their apartment has become too small for the many books and other things they have accumulated during the year. In addition to wanting more space, they also want a house so that they can receive breaks on their income tax, which they do not receive living in an apartment. The Greens also think that a house will be a good financial investment.

The Greens have decided to move into a suburban community. They want a new house and most of the houses within the city limits are rather old. They also feel that they can obtain a larger house for their money in the suburbs than in the city. They have looked at several suburban communities and have decided that they like Lakewood Island better than any of the others. Lakewood Island is an all-White community, which is comprised primarily of lower-middle-class and middle-class residents. There are a few wealthy families in Lakewood Island. But they are the exceptions rather than the rule.

Joan and Henry Green have become frustrated because of the problems they have experienced trying to buy a home in Lakewood Island. Before they go out to look at a house, they carefully study the newspaper ads. When they arrived at the first house in which they were interested, the owner told them that his house had just been sold. A week later they decided to work with a realtor. When they tried to close the deal on the next house they wanted, the realtor told them that the owner had raised the price $10,000 because he had the house appraised since he had put it on the market and had discovered that his selling price was much too low. When the Greens tried to buy a third house in Lakewood Island, the owner told them that he had decided not to sell because he had not received the job in another city that he was almost sure that he would receive when he had put his house up for sale. He explained that the realtor had not removed the ad about his house from the newspaper even though he had told him that he had decided not to sell a week earlier. The realtor the owner had been working with had left the real estate company a few days ago. Henry is bitter and feels that he and his wife are victims of racism and discrimination. Joan believes that Henry is paranoid and that they have been the victims of a series of events that could have happened to anyone, regardless of their race.

1. *What is the main problem in the case?*
2. *What are the values of Joan Green? Henry Green? The Realtor? The Owners? What behaviors show the values you have listed?*
3. *How are the values of these individuals alike and different? Why?: Joan Green, Henry Green, The Realtor, The Owner.*
4. *Why are the values of these individuals alike and different? Joan Green, Henry Green, The Realtor, The Owners.*
5. *What are other values that these individuals could embrace? Joan Green, Henry Green, The Realtor, The Owner.*
6. *What are the possible consequences of the values and actions of each of these individuals? Joan Green, Henry Green, The Realtor, The Owner.*
7. *What should the Greens do?*
8. *Why should the Greens take this action? What are the possible consequences of the actions you stated above?*
9. *What would you do if you were the Greens? Why?*

CONCEPTUAL TEACHING AND CURRICULUM TRANSFORMATION

An important goal of multicultural education is to transform the curriculum so that students develop an understanding of how knowledge is constructed and the extent to which it is influenced by the personal, social, cultural, and gender experiences of knowledge producers (Code, 1991; Collins, 1990; Harding, 1991). Organizing the curriculum around powerful ideas and concepts facilitates the development of teaching strategies and learning experiences that focus on knowledge construction and the development of thinking skills. This chapter describes ways in which a conceptual, transformative, multicultural curriculum can be designed and implemented.

6

EDUCATION FOR FREEDOM

Ann Turnbaugh Lockwood
Interviews James A. Banks

James A. Banks has a reasoned yet eloquent phrase that he uses to encompass the purposes of multicultural education. He maintains that its primary goal—in the broadest sense—is an "education for freedom."

What does that mean? Banks is quick to clarify his phrase. "The goal of multicultural education in the broader sense is an education for freedom," he says. "First, I mean that multicultural education should help students to develop the knowledge, attitudes, and skills to participate in a democratic and free society. Secondly, multicultural education promotes the freedom, abilities, and skills to cross ethnic and cultural boundaries to participate in other cultures and groups." He gives an example. "We empower the Hispanic student to have the freedom to participate in African American culture, and the Jewish student to participate in African American culture—and vice versa. Multicultural education should enable kids to reach beyond their own cultural boundaries."

But in order to cross cultural boundaries and understand other ethnic groups, people must first understand their own cultures. "It's terribly important for kids to be able to participate effectively within their own ethnic and cultural communities," Banks remarks, "to value those communities, but also to realize the limitations of those communities."

A third sense of freedom that multicultural education promotes, Banks says, is providing students with the skills "to participate in social and civic action to make the nation more democratic and free." He adds with some urgency, "By the way, multicultural education is for *all* children, not just for African Americans or Hispanics or Native Americans, but for all students. That's really important, because there are a lot of misconceptions about what multicultural education is. "One misconception," he continues, "is that it is only for African Americans. Another misconception is that it is for inner-city students. It is for everyone."

MULTIPLE VOICES, MULTIPLE PERSPECTIVES

How can the multicultural curriculum help students achieve the goals of an education for freedom? In his response, Banks carefully describes the components that the multicultural curriculum must possess to be successful.

"A multicultural curriculum has several important characteristics," he explains. "One characteristic is to help students understand the nation and the world from diverse ethnic and cultural perspectives. In the multicultural classroom, students hear multiple voices and multiple perspectives. They hear the voice of different ethnic and cultural groups, they hear the voice of the textbook, the voice of the teacher, and the voice of those who have written and are literate."

He adds, "They also hear the voice of those who have merely spoken, such as many individuals within ethnic minority cultures, particularly Native American and African American cultures. Many of the statements from those cultures are oral; just as much of the literature and folk knowledge is oral."

The multicultural curriculum, Banks says, helps students and teachers not only to reformulate the Western-centric curriculum canon but to make what he terms "paradigm shifts." Explaining that a canon in the curriculum refers to a general principle used to choose what knowledge will be taught in schools both in the United States and other Western nations, Banks says that this canon is rarely discussed or questioned. The result, he maintains, is that the curriculum that is in use in most schools largely ignores the experiences of cultures and groups outside the mainstream, such as people of color and women. To illustrate what he means, he provides multiple examples.

"Let's take the concept of the European discovery of America," he says. "This is a very cogent concept that we have been studying for three to four hundred years, because we have had a canon in the curriculum that has included concepts such as the Renaissance and the European discovery of America.

"One of the things a multicultural curriculum does is to help students think about the implications of that concept, namely, that there was a wilderness when the Europeans arrived." He notes dryly, "To discover something implies that it didn't exist before."

TWO OLD WORLD CULTURES MEET

An effective multicultural curriculum encourages students first to consider the Western-centric concept, and then guides them toward a new conception. "Since Native Americans had lived in the Americas for 40,000 years before the Europeans arrived," Banks says, "we could shift the paradigm from the European discovery of America to say that two old world cultures meet. That's a very different way of looking at the same event.

"If you think of two old world cultures meeting, that implies a different set of concepts than the European discovery of America. For one, it implies that the Native Americans had a legitimate ownership of the land when the Europeans arrived. Secondly, it implies that this country wasn't a wilderness when the Europeans arrived, but that people existed here and had established civilizations. The notion of the European discovery of America carries with it a series of concepts, assumptions, and statements that justify the current social, political, and economic structure."

Banks illustrates how the multicultural curriculum can engage students in truly authentic learning and help them make paradigm shifts. He points to ethnic and cultural information that has been neglected in the Western-centric curriculum. "When we talk about Columbus's discovery of America, there is very little talk about Native Americans such as the Taino or the Arawaks. We often don't even mention their names.

"In a lesson I've developed for eighth-graders (this lesson is included in Chapter 5), we ask students to read a selection from Columbus's diary. In that selection Columbus describes the Arawaks as a people 'very deficient in everything.'

"Then we ask the students to read a selection from Fred Olsen's (1974) book, *On The Trail of the Arawaks,* which describes a day in the life of the Arawaks. Of course, they were a preliterate people and therefore didn't leave documents. But Olsen, who was an archeologist, reconstructed a day in the life of the Arawaks. After students have finished the reading, we ask them to *be* an Arawak, to role-play an Arawak and respond to Columbus's diary."

What does this type of exercise accomplish? Its goal, Banks says, is to enable students to see the event from different perspectives. "One of the things we can help the student see is that Columbus indicated that the Arawaks didn't have a language or a god. How do students think the Arawaks would react to this? The Arawaks had a language, but it wasn't Spanish or Italian. They not only had a god, but they had many gods."

To provide another example, Banks moves from Columbus to another portion of American history, the Westward movement. "West to whom?" he asks rhetorically. "When we use that concept, what does it convey?

"It wasn't west to the Sioux; it was the center of the universe, their home. To the Mexicans, it was north. It wasn't west to the Alaskans; it was south. And it wasn't west to the Japanese; it was east. So when you start to look at that concept, what does it mean?

"It's a Eurocentric concept because it was used by the European immigrants who were heading from the Atlantic to the Pacific Ocean. We need to take concepts like that and talk about their multiple meanings."

Banks calls attention to the fact that it will take a long time to change the Western-centric canon, just as it took a long time to establish it. "That's terribly important," he notes.

EVIDENCE TO SUPPORT MULTICULTURAL EDUCATION

Is there sufficient evidence to show that multicultural education achieves its desired effects? Banks believes that the research shows that simple interventions, if conducted early and well enough, can have lasting impact. He cites a review he conducted of research on prejudice reduction and research that asks to what extent multicultural materials can influence students' racial and ethnic attitudes. (For a fuller explication, see Banks, 1991b.)

He describes what he discovered in optimistic terms. "The research is encouraging in the sense that the earlier we start, the more likely we are to intervene successfully. In other words, we *can* be successful, particularly if we start early and if the ethnic content is systemic and ongoing."

One landmark study by Katz and Zalk (1978) illustrates his belief that prejudice can be reduced. "It exemplifies the kind of research that is encouraging," he says. "Katz and Zalk looked at four types of intervention: direct contact, vicarious contact, reinforcement of the color black, and perceptual differentiation of minority group faces."

He emphasizes that each strategy took a relatively brief period of time. "Each strategy lasted only fifteen minutes—and that's a point I want to make. It was a small intervention in terms of time, but it had a cogent impact. The students in the study were elementary students in the New York area, both African American and White, who were high in prejudice.

"Let me talk about what each of these strategies did. For the direct contact strategy, students were given a group activity, such as a puzzle or something they had to complete.

"The vicarious contact strategy consisted of giving students a story that had an ethnic hero. This strategy consisted of the type of contact that would be found in most curriculum materials.

"In the strategy that emphasized reinforcement of the color black, the children were shown a picture of an African American and a White person and asked the question of choice. If the children chose the African American person, they were positively reinforced. If they chose the White person, they weren't punished; they simply weren't reinforced."

Banks stresses the fact that most children have a White bias. "The goal of this research is not to make kids dislike Whites but to lower the White bias. I want to make that clear."

He continues, "The final approach is called perceptual differentiation of minority group faces. Most people, White or African American, tend not to see differentiation in the faces of out-group members as well as they see those of in-group members. Many Whites will tell you that all African Americans look alike, or that they can't tell one Asian from another. To state it scientifically, people tend not to be able to differentiate the faces of out-groups as well as the faces of in-groups.

"In an earlier study, Katz (1973) hypothesized that if she could teach youngsters to differentiate the faces of outgroup members, prejudice would be reduced. Sure enough, through a series of techniques, Katz and Zalk taught African American kids to differentiate the faces of Whites and Whites to differentiate the faces of African Americans."

The end result? "That strategy *did* reduce prejudice," Banks reports. He adds, "By the way, all four of these methods reduced prejudice, and the reduction was effective over a period of four to six months later. The most effective methods were vicarious contact and perceptual differentiation of faces."

He emphasizes, "There is hope. If a fifteen-minute intervention could have this kind of impact, clearly we can make a difference. But again, we have to change the structure of the school and the attitude of the teachers."

CHANGES FOR TEACHERS

What changes do teachers have to undergo to successfully implement a multicultural curriculum? Given the curriculum canon present in most U.S. schools, how likely is it that these changes will occur? Banks believes that changes begin at the personal level first and then extend outward.

He replies, "First, teachers need to examine their own ideologies. Many teachers in our society are highly assimilationist oriented, but they have not examined their ideologies about America and their own conceptions about America.

"I have developed a typology that consists of three ideologies: assimilationist, multicultural, and cultural pluralism (Banks, 1994). Without going into much detail, you can see how they differ. I ask teachers to look at these and to place themselves on the typology. Assimilationist teachers tend to believe that Columbus really *did* discover America and tend to believe that if we teach about differences, that we will disrupt America."

He relates a recent observation. "During an activity that was showing different views of Columbus, one assimilationist teacher said, 'Isn't there anything that is sacred anymore?'"

In addition to examining their own ideologies, teachers need new knowledge about the culture and history of groups, and need to know how to accomplish the same paradigm shifts that their students will need to make.

"I know that's complicated," Banks acknowledges, "and I know that many teachers feel that they will never know enough about all groups. But more than gaining knowledge about the cultural characteristics of specific groups, we need to help teachers attain a process for looking at the American experience so that they can raise questions."

He emphasizes, "We won't know all the answers."

PARADIGM SHIFTS FOR TEACHERS

An important part of the change process is being able to acknowledge that no one will know all the answers—something that may be difficult for teachers who are comfortable in the role of content authority and hesitant to relinquish that position. Banks illustrates the instructional shift that he believes is necessary with an example again related to the Westward movement.

"The teacher should be able to ask: Were there African Americans in the West? If so, how might they have felt?

"I don't think the teacher needs to know how African Americans felt, or needs to know that much about African Americans in the West, but the teacher needs to know that there *were* African Americans in the West and needs to know how to lead an investigation about African Americans in the West."

His next statement is especially emphatic. "The teacher needs to understand the nature of knowledge and needs to understand that knowledge is a process. Teachers can't know everything about every group that was in the West, but we can know how to raise questions about the knowledge we find in textbooks. We need to be able to help students raise questions so that we can do investigations together about the different groups. We don't have to cover all the groups on every topic, but we need to cover samples of content to make the point, such as the European immigrants who were in the West. Think about that. Were they *settlers* or European *immigrants*?"

After posing his question, Banks continues, "Teachers need skills for teaching ethnic content and working with a multicultural population. They need these skills no matter where they teach because the population is changing and because ethnic content contains dilemmas and conflicts that require skills."

Banks explains that new knowledge can frequently become a vehicle through which teachers can examine their own attitudes.

"When I show teachers a film such as *How the West Was Won* or *Honor Lost,* which deals with the Cherokee journey and their forced removal from the Southeast to what was then called Indian territory in Oklahoma, it's a powerful way of dealing with knowledge as well as attitudes.

"Finally, teachers need to examine their own ethnic and cultural history, and their own ethnic journeys. I think many Americans, particularly White Americans, don't believe they have a culture. Once teachers connect to their own cultural experience, it will be a vehicle enabling them to relate to the culture of the kids."

CONTEXTS OF MULTICULTURAL EDUCATION

Should multicultural education differ in various settings, depending on the ethnicity of the predominant population? Banks's response is instantaneous. "The aims of multicultural education should always be the same, regardless of the setting. However, the entry points and methods may have to be contextualized."

To illustrate changes in context, Banks says, "Let's begin with an all-White school, perhaps in a suburb of Madison (Wl). I would argue, though, that even within that all-White school there is diversity. There may be Jews, there may be Poles.

"Now, let's say that we're also looking at an all-African American school in Chicago. There are two contexts. How do we start? The context may imply some differences.

"I would start with each of these groups of students with their own cultural backgrounds. My theory—and there's some evidence to support it—is that we need to start with who we are first.

"What I would do in the all-White school is have the White students look at their own stories."

Banks draws on his own teaching experience to dramatize this example. "I teach an ethnic studies course, primarily to Whites, at the University of Washington. I start out by having my students write a biography of their families. One of the things I argue is that Whites have repressed their own ethnic differences, memories, and identity conflicts. I also argue that the term *White* doesn't help us much and that we need to deconstruct the myth of White homogeneity—the notion that all Whites are the same, that Whites haven't had a struggle."

Banks believes the best progression, in any context, is to start people with their own cultural heritage and move them gradually to other kinds of cultural differences.

"If I were working with African American students in the inner-city of Chicago, I would start them off with their own culture and then move them out. But the goals for the two settings would be the same: to develop multicultural perspectives and to make paradigm shifts. African American kids need to understand White culture in a deep sense, just as White kids need to understand African American culture."

Don't the demands of multicultural education require extremely skilled teachers? Banks agrees that certain skills and attitudes are necessary, but he believes staff development can assist teachers in the change process.

"The most important place to start is staff development, because after having worked in this field for 25 years, I've concluded that multicultural education is primarily a way of thinking. It's a way of asking questions, a way of conceptualizing. I would start with staff development, with new knowledge, with helping teachers ask questions about the materials they have.

"For example, I could have teachers bring their United States history book to a workshop and help them use the materials they have to ask multicultural questions. A multicultural curriculum can be taught with almost any materials if the teachers have the knowledge and the skills to examine the materials critically."

What about special materials? "The key," Banks says reflectively, "is the hearts and minds of teachers and administrators as well, because if teachers don't get support, they give up."

But there are excellent multicultural materials on the market, Banks believes. "For example, there is a new textbook from Globe on the African American experience and a new African American literature book from Holt, Rinehart and Winston. Both of these books cause me just a little concern, though. Maybe they're needed, but they're African American literature and history—which I think is great—but I'm not sure that's sufficient.

"We also need materials to help teachers do comparative studies of ethnic groups, so it seems we've come full circle. In the '60s and early '70s we had materials that focused on specific ethnic groups, such as Black history books and Mexican American history books. And now they are being published again. The challenge is to integrate the African American, Latino, and Asian experience into the mainstream history and literature of the United States.

"However, there are some excellent materials. There are many trade-books that are excellent. I annotate many of those books in my book, *Teaching Strategies for Ethnic Studies* (1991a).

"Clearly, there are supplementary materials, there are hundreds of tradebooks, and of course there are the textbooks, which are better than they were but are not sufficient. They will never be sufficient. The way textbooks are made, they simply are limited in what they can do. We have to supplement textbooks. They are meant to be supplemented.

"But what is needed most is staff development for teachers to develop the knowledge, skills, and attitudes needed to transform their thinking and consequently the school curriculum. We need to teach about knowledge as a construction process, and teachers need to be able to ask kids the questions that enable them to teach knowledge as a construction process. Questions like these: How is knowledge constructed? For whom? For what purpose? What knowledge becomes school knowledge? What purpose does school knowledge serve? Who determines what knowledge becomes popular knowledge, academic knowledge, and school knowledge?" (Banks, 1993a).

ONE NATION UNITED

Some critics of multicultural education argue that focusing on ethnic studies is divisive and causes more tensions between races and ethnic groups. Banks disagrees vehemently.

"Multicultural education is an inclusive and cementing movement, it seems to me, because it attempts to bring various groups that have been on the margins of society to the center of society. Rather than divisive, it's inclusive."

He is eager to elucidate his argument. "A lot of people are on the margins of society because of their race, class, gender, or sexual orientation. Multicultural education is about bringing them to the center, making one nation from many people. That is consistent with the nation's motto, 'E Pluribus Unum.'

"To do that we have to validate their experiences and these groups have to see themselves as part of the whole. Their experience must be mirrored in the commonwealth and in the mainstream society.

"Critics who think multicultural education is divisive are assuming that the United States is now *united* in a sociological sense. I *challenge* that assumption," Banks says with some passion. "I would argue that we are not united now, that the nation is highly divided along class, racial and ethnic lines, and that multicultural education is working to bring greater unity among the nation's diverse groups of people.

"Look at the class divisions in our society, the gender differences! We're not united!

"The best way for groups to forget about particularistic differences is for those groups to be included in the commonwealth. Multicultural education is about inclusion, and that's how you bring about an overarching commonwealth, through inclusion in the curriculum, in public policy. You can't impose inclusion. It has to be participatory. People on the margins of society have to participate in shaping the vision of the commonwealth if they are really to feel included, so I would challenge the notion that we are already united, and argue that multicultural education is a uniting and cementing force."

7

MULTICULTURAL BENCHMARKS

In this chapter, I summarize and highlight the major components of multicultural education and describe benchmarks that you can use to determine the extent to which your school is multicultural, steps that need to be taken to make it more reflective of cultural diversity, and ways to enhance your school's multicultural climate on a continuing basis. Figure 7–1 summarizes the multicultural benchmarks discussed in this chapter.

A POLICY STATEMENT

Your school district needs a policy statement on multicultural education that clearly communicates the board of education's commitment to creating and maintaining schools in which students from both gender groups and from diverse racial, ethnic, social-class and cultural groups will have an equal opportunity to learn.

A cogent board of education policy statement will serve several important purposes. It will give legitimacy to multicultural education in the district and thus facilitate the establishment of programs and practices that foster cultural diversity and equal educational opportunities for all students. A board policy statement will also communicate to parents and the public-at-large that multicultural education is a priority in the district.

The board policy statement should include a rationale or justification for multicultural education and guidelines that can be used by the

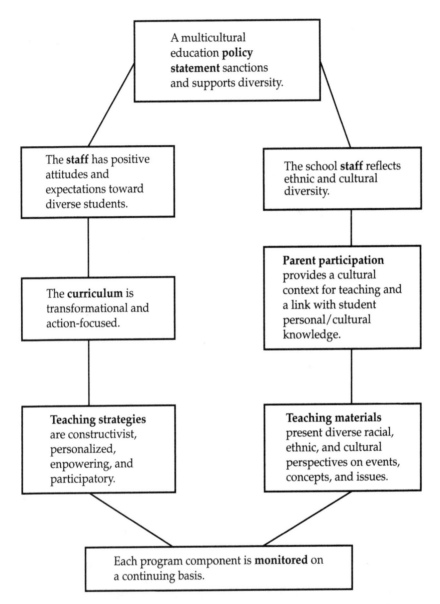

FIGURE 7–1 **Multicultural Benchmarks for Assessing and Maintaining an Effective Multicultural School**

professional and supportive staffs in the district to develop and implement a comprehensive multicultural education plan. In the policy statement adopted by the New York (City) Board of Education (1989), the rationale includes these statements:

> *WHEREAS, people from all parts of the world live and work in New York City, necessitating a multicultural education which fosters inter-group knowledge and understanding and equips students to function effectively in a global society; and*
>
> *WHEREAS, multicultural education values cultural pluralism and rejects the view that schools should seek to melt away cultural differences or merely tolerate cultural diversity; rather, multicultural education accepts cultural diversity as a valuable resource that should be preserved and extended. . . .*

The full text of the New York Board of Education policy statement on multicultural education is found in Appendix B, pages 109 to 111.

Your school district can model its multicultural policy statement on the one developed by the New York Board of Education. Other helpful resources for multicultural education rationales are the position statements developed by national professional organizations, such as the *Curriculum Guidelines for Multicultural Education,* a policy statement adopted by the National Council for the Social Studies (Banks et al., 1992). The rationale for the NCSS guidelines includes these principles:

1. Ethnic and cultural diversity should be recognized and respected at the individual, group, and societal levels.
2. Ethnic and cultural diversity provides a basic for societal enrichment, cohesiveness, and survival.
3. Equality of opportunity should be afforded to members of all ethnic and cultural groups.
4. Ethnic and cultural identification should be optional for individuals.

THE SCHOOL STAFF

The school staff—including administrators, teachers, counselors, and the supportive staff—should reflect the racial and cultural diversity in U.S. society. The people students see working and interacting in the school environment teach them important lessons about the attitudes of adults toward racial and ethnic diversity. Students need to see administrators, teachers, and counselors from different racial and ethnic backgrounds in order for them to believe that our society values and respects people from different ethnic, racial, and cultural groups. If most of the people students see in powerful and important positions in the school environment are from the dominant racial group, they will have a difficult time developing democratic racial attitudes, no matter how cogent are the words we speak about racial equality. Students' experiences speak much more powerfully than the words they hear.

School districts should develop and implement a strong policy for the recruitment, hiring, and promotion of people from different racial and ethnic groups. Because the percentage of some groups of color—such as African Americans and Mexican Americans—entering and completing college has declined or remained at low levels in recent years (Carter & Wilson, 1991), the pool of ethnic minority candidates from which school districts can recruit is likewise declining. Consequently, school districts need to develop and implement innovative and experimental projects to increase the number of students of color who are entering the teaching profession. A number of school districts have implemented or are participating in such innovative projects. Some of these projects consist of early identification programs in which promising students of color in high school are identified and given incentives for choosing teaching as a career.

STAFF ATTITUDES AND EXPECTATIONS

School districts need to implement continuing staff development programs that help practicing educators to develop high expectations for low-income and minority students and to better understand the cultural experiences of these students. An increasing percentage of students in school today are from single-parent homes, have parents with special needs, and have cultural experiences that are dissimilar in significant ways from that of their teachers (Graham, 1992; Hodgkinson, 1991).

Many of these students have health, motivational, and educational needs that often challenge the most gifted and dedicated teachers. Yet many of these students are academically gifted and talented, although their gifts and talents are often not immediately evident and are not revealed by standardized mental ability tests. Their academic gifts and talents are often obscured by skill deficits. Teachers need special training to develop the skills and sensitivities needed to perceive the hidden and underdeveloped talent and abilities of a significant number of minority and low-income students. Only when they are able to perceive the unrealized talent and potential of these students will teachers be able to increase their expectations for them.

Gardner's (1983) theory of *multiple intelligences* can help teachers to reconceptualize the concept of intelligence and to develop a broader view of human ability. This broad view will enable them to see more intellectual strengths in culturally different and low-income students.

Creating successful experiences for students of color will enable them to develop a high self-concept of academic ability as well as enable their teachers to increase their academic expectations for them (Brookover & Erickson, 1969). Student behavior and teacher expectations are related in an interactive way. The more teachers expect from students academically, the more they are likely to achieve; the more academically successful students are, the higher teacher expectations are likely to be for them (Brophy & Good, 1970; Rosenthal & Jacobson, 1968).

THE CURRICULUM

The school curriculum should be reformed so that students will view concepts, events, issues, and problems from different ethnic perspectives and points of view (Banks, 1991a). Reconceptualizing the curriculum and making ethnic content an integral part of a transformed curriculum should be distinguished from merely adding ethnic content to the curriculum. Ethnic content can be added to the curriculum without transforming it or changing its basic assumptions, perspectives, and goals.

Content about Native Americans can be added to a Eurocentric curriculum that teaches students that Columbus discovered America. In such a curriculum, the students will read about Columbus's view of the Indians when he "discovered" them. In a transformed curriculum in which content about Indians is an integral part, the interaction of Columbus and the Indians would not be conceptualized as Columbus "discovering" the Indians. Rather, students would read about the culture of the Arawak Indians as it existed in the late 1400s (Olsen, 1974), the journey of Columbus, and the meeting of the aboriginal American and European cultures in the Caribbean in 1492.

"Discovery" is not an accurate way to conceptualize and view the interaction of Columbus and the Arawaks unless this interaction is viewed exclusively from the point of view of Columbus and other Europeans. "The Meeting of Two Old World Cultures" is a more appropriate way to describe the Arawak-Columbus encounter. It is imperative that the encounter be viewed from the perspectives of the Arawaks or Tainos (Golden et al., 1991; Ponce de Leon, 1992; Stannard, 1992), in addition to that of Columbus and the Europeans (Morison, 1974).

The multicultural curriculum not only helps students to view issues and problems from diverse ethnic perspectives and points of view, it is also conceptual, interdisciplinary, and decision-making focused (see Chapter 5). *It helps students to make decisions on important issues and to take effective civic action* (Banks with Clegg, 1990).

The multicultural curriculum is a dynamic process; it is not possible to create a multicultural curriculum, hand it to teachers, and claim that a multicultural curriculum exists in the district. The teacher's role in its implementation is an integral part of a multicultural curriculum. The teacher mediates the curriculum with his or her values, perspectives, and teaching styles. Although multicultural materials are essential for implementing a multicultural curriculum, they are ineffective when used by a teacher who lacks a knowledge base in multicultural education or who does not have positive and clarified attitudes toward a range of ethnic and racial groups. A well-designed, continuing staff development program is essential for the development and implementation of an effective multicultural curriculum.

An effective preservice teacher education program is also essential for the successful implementation of multicultural education in the schools. School districts should demand that teacher education institutions have a strong multicultural education component in their programs as a condition for the employment of their graduates. The National Council for the Accreditation of Teacher Education has taken a leadership role in multicultural education by requiring its members to implement components, courses, and programs in multicultural education (National Council for the Accreditation of Teacher Education, 1977). A large number of the nation's teacher education institutions are members of NCATE.

TEACHING STRATEGIES

The multicultural curriculum should be implemented with teaching strategies that are involvement oriented, interactive, personalized, and cooperative. The teacher should listen to and legitimize the voices of students from different racial, cultural, and gender groups. Multicultural content is inherently emotive, personal, conflictual, and involving. Consequently, it is essential that students be given ample opportunities to express their feelings and emotions, to interact with their peers and classmates, and to express rage or pride when multicultural issues are discussed.

Teacher-centered instruction has serious disadvantages when teaching any kind of content. However, it is especially inappropriate when teaching multicultural content, an area in which diversity is valued and different perspectives are an integral part of the content.

TEACHING MATERIALS

School districts need to develop and implement a policy for selecting teaching materials that describe the historical and contemporary experiences of various ethnic and cultural groups and that present issues, problems, and concepts from the perspectives of these groups. It is not sufficient for textbooks and other teaching materials to merely include content about various ethnic and cultural groups. The content about ethnic and cultural groups should be an integral part of the textbook or presentation and not an add-on or appendage. It is not uncommon for content about people of color and women to be added to a textbook in a special section, as a special feature, or with photographs.

When ethnic content is placed in teaching materials primarily as add-ons or appendages, the text or presentation has not been reconceptualized or reformed in a way that will allow students to rethink the American experience, to challenge their current assumptions, or to develop new perspectives and insights on U.S. history and culture. If ethnic content is added to teaching materials and viewed from Anglo-centric perspectives and points of view—which often happens—ethnic stereotypes and misconceptions held by students are likely to be reinforced rather than reduced. How ethnic content is integrated into textbooks and other teaching materials is as important, if not more important, than whether or not it is included.

DISPROPORTIONALITY

A major goal of multicultural education is to create equal educational opportunities for students from different racial, ethnic, and social-class groups (see Chapter 3). The gaps in academic achievement, dropout, and graduation rates for students from different racial and income groups are enormous in most school districts. Each school district needs to determine the gaps in academic achievement, dropout rates, and graduation rates for students from different racial and income groups. Each district also needs to develop a comprehensive and well-conceptualized plan for closing these gaps.

Special attention should also be given to the proportion of students of color that is expelled or suspended from school, and the percentage that is enrolled in special education and in classes for gifted students (Zigmond, 1992). In most school districts, students of color—especially males—are overrepresented among the students who are suspended from school and in classes for the mentally retarded (Reschly, 1988). However, these students are usually underrepresented in classes for gifted students.

A goal of each school district should be to have students from different racial and social-class groups represented in special education and in gifted classes roughly equal to their percentage in their district's population. This means that the percentage of students of color in special education would be reduced and their percentage in classes for gifted students would increase in most school districts.

PARENT INVOLVEMENT

Because of the enormity of the problems faced by schools today, it is not likely that the school can succeed in its major mission—helping students to attain academic skills and to become citizens of a democratic society—unless it can solicit the support of parents and the public-at-large (Graham, 1992). However, soliciting the support of parents is a tremendous challenge for schools in today's society. Increasingly within the United States both parents work outside the home. According to *Education Week* (Here They Come, Ready or Not, May 14, 1986), fewer than 5 percent of U.S. households now conform to the standard-model family of past decades—a working father, mother at home, and two or more school-age children.

Other institutions are increasingly taking on functions that were in the past the primary responsibility of families. Because of the tremendous changes within U.S. society, we need to rethink the idea of parent involvement and reconceptualize ways in which parents can support the school, given the other demands now being made on their time (Comer, 1980). Asking a parent to provide a place for his or her child to study, to monitor the child's TV watching, and to restrict it to one hour per day may be a limited involvement, but it may be the only kind of parent involvement that the school can realistically expect from many parents who care deeply about their chidlren's education.

Educators should be careful not to equate noninvolvement in traditional ways in school as lack of parent interest or lack of participation. Also, many parents are reluctant to get involved with schools because they lack a sense of empowerment and believe that their opinion will not matter anyway. Other parents are reluctant to become involved with schools because of their painful memories of their own school days.

School districts should conceptualize and implement a program for involving parents in school that is consistent with the changing characteristics of families, parents, and society (Graham, 1992; Hodgkinson, 1992).

MONITORING

The successful implementation and improvement of a multicultural education program within a school or district requires an effective monitoring plan. Ways must be developed to determine whether the multicultural education goals established by the board of education are being attained, steps that need to be taken to close the gap between the goals and actual program implementation, and incentives that are needed to motivate people in the district to participate in the efforts being undertaken to attain the district's multicultural education goals and objectives.

An effective monitoring program may include (1) classroom visitations to determine the extent to which the content and strategies used by teachers are consistent with the cultural characteristics of students, (2) examination of standardized test scores disaggregated by race and social class, and (3) examination of the percentage of students of color who are suspended, who are dropouts, and who are classified as mentally retarded and gifted.

The monitoring program should not focus on specific individuals, such as teachers and principals, but should be systemic and focus on the total school as a unit. A systemic approach to monitoring will weaken resistance to a comprehensive monitoring program as well as reinforce the idea that multicultural education is a shared responsibility of the school and that everyone within the school building has a stake in its successful implementation, including the principal, teachers, as well as other members of the professional and support staffs, such as the secretary, the custodian, and the bus driver.

An effective and well-conceptualized monitoring program will provide the feedback needed to determine whether the benchmarks described in this chapter are being realized in your school and steps that need to be taken to ensure the ongoing improvement of its multicultural climate. The *Multicultural Evaluation Checklist* in Appendix C is designed to help you assess the environment of your school and to plan and implement action to make it more consistent with the multicultural realities of the United States and the world.

GLOSSARY

Afrocentric Explanations, cultural characteristics, teaching materials, and other factors related to the heritages, histories, and cultures of people of African descent who live in the United States and in other parts of the world.

Anglocentric Explanations, cultural characteristics, teaching materials, and other factors related the heritages, histories, and cultures of Whites in the United States of British descent.

Canon A standard or criteria used to define, select, and evaluate knowledge in the school and university curriculum within a nation. The list of book-length works or readings selected using the standard is also described as the canon. Historically in the United States, the canon that has dominated the curriculum has been Eurocentric and male oriented.

Culture The ideations, symbols, behaviors, values, and beliefs that are shared by a human group. Culture may also be defined as the symbols, institutions or other components of human societies that are created by human groups to meet their survival needs.

Ethnic Group A group that shares a common history, a sense of peoplehood and identity, values, behavioral characteristics, and a communication system. The members of an ethnic group usually view their group as distinct and separate from other cultural groups within a society. Ethnic groups within the United States include Anglo Americans, Irish Americans, Polish Americans, and German Americans.

Ethnic Minority Group An ethnic group that has unique behavioral and/or racial characteristics that enable other groups to easily identify its members. These groups are often a numerical minority within the nation-state and the victims of institutionalized discrimination. Jewish Americans are an example of an ethnic group differentiated on the basic of cultural and religious characteristics. African Americans, Mexican Americans, and Japanese Americans are differentiated on the basis of both biological and cultural characteristics.

Ethnic-Specific Programs, curricula, and educational policies that focus on one designated ethnic group, such as Anglo Americans or Asian Americans, rather than on a range of ethnic and cultural groups.

Ethnic Studies The scientific and humanistic study of the histories, cultures, and experiences of ethnic groups within the United States and in other societies.

Eurocentric Explanations, cultural characteristics, teaching materials, and other factors related to the heritages, histories, and cultures of people of European descent who live in the United States and in other nations.

Global Education The study of the cultures, institutions, and interconnectedness of nations outside of the United States. Global education is often confused with multicultural education. Multicultural education deals with educational issues in the United States or within another nation. Global education deals with issues, problems, and developments outside of the United States or outside another nation.

Knowledge Construction The process that helps students understand how social, behavioral, and natural scientists create knowledge, and how their implicit cultural assumptions, frames of references, perspectives, cultural contexts, and biases influence the knowledge they construct. Knowledge construction teaching strategies, which are constructivist, involve students in activities that enable them to create their own interpretations of the past, present, and future.

Multicultural Education An educational reform movement whose major goal is to restructure curricula and educational institutions so that students from diverse social-class, racial, and ethnic groups—as well as both gender groups—will experience equal educational opportunities.

Multiculturalists A group of theorists, researchers, and educators who believe that the curricula within the nation's schools, colleges, and universities should be reformed so that they reflect the experiences and perspectives of the diverse cultures and groups in U.S. society.

Multiethnic Education An educational reform movement designed to restructure educational institutions so that students from diverse ethnic groups, such as Asian Americans, Native Americans, and Hispanics, will experience equal educational opportunities.

Paradigm An interrelated set of facts, concepts, generalizations, and theories that attempt to explain human behavior or a social phenomenon and that imply policy and action. A paradigm, which is also a set of explanations, has specific goals, assumptions, and values that can be described. Paradigms compete with one another in the arena of ideas and educational policy. Explanations such as *at-risk students, culturally deprived students,* and *culturally different students* are paradigms.

Paradigm Shift Describes the process that occurs when an individual accepts and internalizes an explanation or theory to explain a phenomenon or event that differs substantially from the one that he or she previously had internalized. An example is when an individual who previously believed that Columbus discovered America now views the Columbus-Arawak encounter as the meeting of two old world cultures.

People of Color A term use to refer to racial groups in the United States that have historically experienced institutionalized discrimination and racism because of their physical characteristics. These groups include African Americans, Asian Americans, Hispanics, Native Americans, and Native Hawaiians.

Powerful Ideas Key concepts or themes—such as culture, socialization, power, and discrimination—that are used to organized lessons, units, and courses. In conceptual teaching, instruction focuses on helping students to see relationships and to derive principles and generalizations.

Transformative Curriculum A curriculum that challenges the basic assumptions and implicit values of the Eurocentric, male-dominated curriculum institutionalized in U.S. schools, colleges, and universities. It helps students to view concepts, events, and situations from diverse racial, ethnic, gender, and social-class perspectives. The transformative curriculum also helps students to construct their own interpretations of the past, present, and future.

Western Traditionalists Social scientists, historians, and other scholars who argue that the European Western tradition should be at the center of the curriculum in U.S. schools, colleges, and universities because of the cogent influence that Western ideals have had on the development of the United States.

Appendix A

THE ACADEMIC KNOWLEDGE COMPONENT OF MULTICULTURAL EDUCATION: A BIBLIOGRAPHY

Race, Culture and Ethnicity

Acuña, Rodolfo. (1988). *Occupied America: A History of Chicanos*. (3rd ed.). New York: Harper & Row.

Alba, Richard D. (1985). *Italian Americans: Into the Twilight of Ethnicity*. Englewood Cliffs, NJ: Prentice Hall.

Alba, Richard D. (1990). *Ethnic Identity: The Transformation of White America*. New Haven, CT: Yale University Press.

Allport, Gordon W. (1954). *The Nature of Prejudice*. Reading, MA: Addison-Wesley.

Aptheker, Herbert (Ed.). (1973). *The Published Writings of W. E. B. DuBois* (38 volumes). Kraus International Publications, Route 100, Millwood, New York 10546. Phone: 914-762-2200. (See especially *Black Reconstruction*, 1935).

Banks, James A. (1991). *Teaching Strategies for Ethnic Studies* (5th ed.). Boston: Allyn and Bacon.

Forbes, Jack D. (1960). *Apache, Navaho and Spaniard*. Norman: University of Oklahoma Press.

Franklin, John Hope, and Moss, Alfred A., Jr. (1988). *From Slavery to Freedom: A History of Negro Americans* (6th ed.) New York: Knopf.

Glazer, Nathan (1972). *American Judaism* (2nd ed., rev.). Chicago: University of Chicago Press.

Jennings, Francis. (1975). *The Invasion of America: Indians, Colonialism, and the Cant of Conquest*. New York: Norton.

Mindel, Charles H., & Habenstein, Robert W. (Eds.). (1981). *Ethnic Families in America: Patterns and Variations* (2nd ed.). New York: Elsevier.

Myrdal, Gunnar, with the assistance of Richard Sterner and Arnold Rose. (1944). *An American Dilemma: The Negro Problem and Modern Democracy*. New York: Harper and Brothers.

Nash, Gary B. (1982). *Red, White and Black: The Peoples of Early America* (2nd ed.). Englewood Cliffs, NJ: Prentice Hall.

Novak, Michael. (1971). *The Rise of the Unmeltable Ethnics.* New York: Macmillan.

Quinley, Harold E., & Glock, Charles Y. (1979). *Anti-Semitism in America.* New York: Free Press.

Rodriguez, Clara E. (1989). *Puerto Ricans Born in the U.S.A.* Boston: Unwin Hyman.

Takaki, Ronald T. (1979). *Iron Cages: Race and Culture in Nineteenth-Century America.* Seattle: University of Washington Press.

Takaki, Ronald. (1989). *Strangers from a Different Shore: A History of Asian Americans.* Boston: Little, Brown.

Takaki, Ronald. (1993). *A Different Mirror: A History of Multicultural America.* Boston: Little, Brown.

Thernstrom, Stephan, Orlov, Ann, & Handlin, Oscar. (Eds.). (1980). *Harvard Encyclopedia of American Ethnic Groups.* Cambridge, MA: Harvard University Press.

Zinn, Howard. (1980). *A People's History of the United States.* New York: Harper & Row.

Williams, George Washington. (1883). *History of the Negro Race in America* (Volumes I and II). Ayer Company, 50 Northwestern Drive, Salem, NH 03079.

Woodson, Carter G. (1933). *The Mis-Education of the Negro.* Washington, DC: The Associated Publishers.

Gender and Culture

Anzaldúa, Gloria. (1987). *Borderlands: The New Mestiza.* San Francisco: Spinsters/Aunt Lute Book Company.

Anzaldúa, Gloria. (Ed.). (1990). *Making Face, Making Soul: Haciendo Caras.* San Francisco: Aunt Lute Foundation Books.

Code, Lorraine. (1991). *What Can She Know: Feminist Theory and the Construction of Knowledge.* Ithaca, NY: Cornell University Press.

Collins, Patricia Hill. (1990). *Black Feminist Thought: Knowledge, Consciousness, and the Politics of Empowerment.* New York: Routledge.

Farganis, Sondra. (1986). *The Social Construction of the Femine Character.* Totowa, NJ: Rowman and Littlefield.

Giddings, Paula. (1984). *When and Where I Enter: The Impact of Black Women on Race and Sex in America.* New York: Bantam.

Harding, Sandra. (1986). *The Science Question in Feminism.* Ithaca, NY: Cornell University Press.

Harding Sandra. (1991). *Whose Science? Whose Knowledge? Thinking from Women's Lives.* Ithaca, NY: Cornell University Press.

Hine, Darlene Clark. (Ed.). (1990). *Black Women in United States History: From Colonial Times to the Present* (16 Volumes). Carlson Publishing, P.O. Box 023350, Brooklyn, NY 11202-0067. Phone 1-800-336-7460.

hooks, bell. (1984). *Feminist Theory: From Margin to Center.* Boston: South End Press.

Lerner, Gerda. (1979). *The Majority Finds Its Past: Placing Women in History.* New York: Oxford University Press.

Minnich, Elizabeth K. (1990). *Transforming Knowledge.* Philadelphia: Temple University Press.

Appendix B

BOARD OF EDUCATION, CITY OF NEW YORK

Statement of Policy on Multicultural Education and Promotion of Positive Intergroup Relations November 9, 1989 (Amended)

The Chancellor submits the following resolutions for adoption:

WHEREAS, all students are entitled to a quality education which enables them to achieve to their fullest potential; and

WHEREAS, people from all parts of the world live and work in New York city, necessitating a multicultural education which fosters intergroup knowledge and understanding and equips students to function effectively in a global society; and

WHEREAS, multicultural education values cultural pluralism and rejects the view that schools should seek to melt away cultural differences or merely tolerate cultural diversity; rather, multicultural education accepts cultural diversity as a valuable resource that should be preserved and extended; and

WHEREAS, on February 15, 1989 the Board of Education accepted the report and recommendations of the Human Relations *Task Force* insofar as it identified the need for a comprehensive multicultural education program to help foster positive intergroup relations and to eliminate bias of all forms; and

WHEREAS, this resolution extends the policy for Intergroup Relations established by the Board of Education on November 20, 1985 directing the chancellor to "take appropriate steps to bring about the elimination of practices which foster attitudes and/or actions leading to discrimination against students, parents, or school personnel on the basis of race, color, religion, national origin, gender, age, sexual orientation and/or handicapping condition;" now be it therefore

RESOLVED, that the New York City Board of Education, by adoption of this resolution, hereby ratifies a policy of multicultural education and commits itself and its resources to providing an education to achieve the following goals:

To develop an appreciation and understanding of the heritage of students' and staffs' own ethnic, racial, cultural and linguistic groups.

To promote and foster intergroup understanding, awareness, and appreciation by students and staff of the diverse ethnic, racial, cultural and linguistic groups represented in the New York City public schools and the general population.

To enhance New York City youngsters' self-worth and self-respect.

To encourage a variety of teaching strategies to address differences in learning styles.

To identify the impact of racism and other barriers to acceptance of differences.

To develop opportunities for all students to become bilingual and proficient in at least two languages.

To develop a multicultural perspective (interpreting history and culture form a variety of perspectives).

To analyze human rights violations in our global society and the progress made in obtaining human rights.

To develop an appreciation of the cultural and historical contributions of a variety of racial and ethnic groups to the growth of the United States and world civilizations.

To develop the human relations skills needed in interpersonal and intergroup relations, as well as conflict resolution, with a special emphasis on conflict arising from bias and discrimination based on race, color, religion, national origin, gender, age, sexual orientation, and/or handicapping condition; and be it further

RESOLVED, that the Chancellor shall develop procedures and guidelines for textbook selection; shall review all textbooks and instructional materials to ensure that they are free of stereotypical views of any group whether expressed or implied, by statement, visual image or by omission; and shall, when necessary, develop supplementary material when commercially available material fails to meet guidelines for comprehensive and accurate instruction; and be it further

RESOLVED, that the Chancellor shall submit to the Board a comprehensive multicultural education plan which shall include guidelines and procedures for program, staff, and curriculum development.

EXPLANATION

This resolution formalizes the recognition by the Chancellor and the New York City Board of Education of the need for a multicultural education initiative.

The commitment to multicultural education will permeate every aspect of educational policy, including counseling programs, assessment and testing, curriculum and instruction, representative staffing at all levels, and teaching materials. Cultural diversity is to be viewed as an enrichment to learning and not as a deficit.

There will be opportunities for community-based organizations, cultural institutions, and institutions of higher learning to cooperate in developing and maintaining multicultural education in the schools.

The input and cooperation of parents and students are of critical importance in the design and implementation of multicultural education programs. Therefore, a high-priority will be placed on their involvement in all aspects of this initiative.

Staff development which emphasizes the philosophy, attitudes, skills, knowledge, practices, and procedures essential to a sound program of multicultural education is to be provided on continuous, consistent basis for all staff involved in the education process. There must be multicultural staff recruitment and development to aid in the implementation of this policy.

A TRUE COPY OF AMENDED AND CORRECTED RESOLUTION(S) ADOPTED
BY THE BOARD OF EDUCATION ON NOV. 15, 1989
ASSISTANT SECRETARY, BOARD OF EDUCATION

Appendix C

A MULTICULTURAL EDUCATION EVALUATION CHECKLIST

Criteria Questions

Rating

Criteria Questions	Strongly ⟵————————⟶ Hardly at all		
1. Does school policy reflect the ethnic, cultural, and gender diversity in U.S. society?			
2. Is the total school culture (including the hidden curriculum) multiethnic and multicultural?			
3. Do the learning styles favored by the school reflect the learning styles of the students?			
4. Does the school reflect and sanction the range of languages and dialects spoken by the students and within the larger society?			
5. Does the school involve parents from diverse ethnic and cultural groups in school activities, programs, and planning?			

Criteria Questions   Rating

                    Strongly <————————————> *Hardly at all*

6. Does the counseling program of the school reflect the ethnic diversity in U.S. society?			
7. Are the testing procedures used by the school multicultural and ethnically fair?			
8. Are instructional materials examined for ethnic, cultural, and gender bias?			
9. Are the formalized curriculum and course of study multiethnic and multicultural? Do they help students to view events, situations, and concepts from diverse ethnic and cultural perspectives and points of view?			
10. Do the teaching styles and motivational systems in the school reflect the ethnic and cultural diversity of the student body?			
11. Are the attitudes, perceptions, beliefs, and behavior of the total staff ethnically and racially sensitive?			
12. Does the school have systematic, comprehensive, mandatory, and continuing multicultural staff development programs?			
13. Is the school staff (administrative, instructional, counseling, and supportive) multiethnic and multicultural?			

Criteria Questions   Rating

	Strongly ⟵―――――――――――――⟶ Hardly at all		
14. Is the total atmosphere of the school positively responsive to racial, ethnic, cultural, and language differences?			
15. Do school assemblies and holidays reflect the ethnic and cultural diversity in U.S. society?			
16. Does the school lunch program prepare meals that reflect the range of ethnic foods eaten in the U.S.?			
17. Do the bulletin boards, physical education program, music, and other displays and activities in the school reflect ethnic and cultural diversity?			

Source: Adapted from James A. Banks, "Multiethnic Education and School Reform." In L. V. Edinger, P. L. Houts, & D. V. Meyer (Eds.) *Education in the 80's: Curricular Challenges.* Washington, DC: National Education Association, 1981, pp. 121–122. Copyright 1981, National Education Association. Reprinted with permission.

Appendix D

TEN QUICK WAYS TO ANALYZE CHILDREN'S BOOKS FOR SEXISM AND RACISM

Both in school and out, young children are exposed to racist and sexist attitudes. These attitudes—expressed over and over in books and in other media—gradually distort their perceptions until stereotypes and myths about minorities and women are accepted as reality. It is difficult for a librarian or teacher to convince children to question society's attitudes. But if a child can be shown how to detect racism and sexism in a book, the child can proceed to transfer the perception to wider areas. The following ten guidelines are offered as a starting point in evaluation of children's books from this perspective.

1. Check the Illustrations

Look for Stereotypes. A stereotype is an oversimplified generalization about a particular group, race, or sex that usually carries derogatory implications. Some infamous (overt) stereotypes of Blacks are the happy-go-lucky, watermelon-eating Sambo and the fat, eye-rolling "mammy"; of Chicanos, the sombrero-wearing peon, or fiesta-loving, macho bandito; of Asian Americans, the inscrutable, slant-eyed "Oriental"; of Native Americans, the naked savage or "primitive" craftsperson and his "squaw"; of Puerto Ricans, the switchblade-toting, teenage gang member; of women, the completely domesticated mother, the demure, doll-loving little girl, or the wicked stepmother. Although you may not

Reprinted by permission from *Guidelines for Selecting Bias-Free Textbooks and Storybooks*. New York: Council on Interracial Books for Children, PO Box 1263, New York, NY 10023.

always find stereotypes in the blatant forms described, look for variations that in any way demean or ridicule characters because of their race or sex.

Look for Tokenism. If there are minority characters in the illustrations, do they look just like Whites except for being tinted or colored in? Do all minority faces look stereotypically alike, or are they depicted as genuine individuals with distinctive features?

Who's Doing What? Do the illustrations depict minorities in subservient and passive roles or in leadership and action roles? Are males the active "doers" and females the inactive observers?

2. Check the Story Line

The liberation movements have led publishers to weed out many insulting passages, particularly from stories with Black themes and from books depicting female characters; however, racist and sexist attitudes still find expression in less obvious ways. The following checklist suggests some of the subtle, covert forms of bias to watch for.

Standard for Success. Does it take "White" behavior standards for a minority person to "get ahead"? Is "making it" in the dominant White society projected as the only ideal? To gain acceptance and approval, do third-world persons have to exhibit extraordinary qualities—excel in sports, get A grades, and so on? In friendships between White and third-world children, is it the third-world child who does most of the understanding and forgiving?

Resolution of Problems. How are problems presented, conceived, and resolved in the story? Are minority people considered to be "the problem"? Are the oppressions faced by minorities and women represented as casually related to an unjust society? Are the reasons for poverty and oppression explained, or are they accepted as inevitable? Does the story line encourage passive acceptance or active resistance? Is a particular problem that is faced by a minority person resolved through the benevolent intervention of a White person?

Role of Women. Are the achievements of girls and women based on their own initiative and intelligence, or are they due to their good looks or to their relationship with boys? Are sex roles incidental or critical to characterization and plot? Could the same story be told if the sex roles were reversed?

3. Look at the Life-Styles

Are third-world persons and their setting depicted in such a way that they contrast unfavorably with the unstated norm of White, middle-class suburbia? If the minority group in question is depicted as "different," are negative value judgments implied? Are minorities depicted exclusively in ghettos, barrios, or migrant camps? If the illustrations and text attempt to depict another culture, do they go beyond oversimplifications and offer genuine insights into another life-style? Look for inaccuracy and inappropriateness in the depiction of other cultures. Watch for instances of the "quaint-natives-in-costume" syndrome (most noticeable in areas like clothing and custom, but extending to behavior and personality traits as well).

4. Weigh the Relationships Between People

Do the Whites in the story possess the power, take the leadership, and make the important decisions? Do minorities and females function in essentially supporting, subservient roles?

How are family relationships depicted? In Black families, is the mother always dominant? In Latino families, are there always lots of children? If the family is separated, are societal conditions—unemployment, poverty—cited among the reasons for the separation?

5. Note the "Her-os"

For many years, books showed only "safe" minority heros—those who avoided serious conflict with the White establishment of their time. Minority groups today are insisting on the right to define their own heros (of both sexes) based on their own concepts and struggles for justice.

When minority heros do appear, are they admired for the same qualities that have made White heros famous, or because what they have done has benefited White people? Ask this question: Whose interests is a particular hero really serving? The interests of the hero's own people? Or the interests of White people?

6. Consider the Effects on a Child's Self-Image

Are norms established which limit any child's aspirations and self-concepts? What effect can it have on third-world children to be continuously bombarded with images of the color white as the ultimate in beauty, cleanliness, virtue, and so on, and the color black as evil, dirty, menacing, and the like? Does the book reinforce or counteract positive associations with the color white and negative associations with the color black?

What happens to a girl's self-image when she reads that boys perform all of the brave and important deeds? What about a girl's self-esteem if she is not "fair" of skin and slim of body? In a particular story, is there one or more persons with whom a minority child can readily identify to a positive and constructive end?

7. Consider the Author's or Illustrator's Background

Analyze the biographical material on the jacket flap or the back of the book. If a story deals with a minority theme, what qualifies the author or illustrator to deal with the subject? If the author and illustrator are not members of the minority being written about, is there anything in their background that would specifically recommend them as the creators of this book?

8. Check out the Author's Perspective

No author can be entirely objective. All authors write from a cultural as well as personal context. Children's books in the past have traditionally come from authors who were White and who were members of the middle class, with one result being that a single ethnocentric perspective has dominated children's literature in the United States. With any book in question, read carefully to determine whether the direction of the author's perspective substantially weakens or strengthens the value of his or her written work. Is the perspective patriarchal or feminist? Is it solely Eurocentric or do third-world perspectives also surface?

9. Watch for Loaded Words

A word is loaded when it has offensive overtones. Examples of loaded adjectives (usually racist) are *savage, primitive, conniving, lazy, superstitious, treacherous, wily, crafty, inscrutable, docile,* and *backward*.

Look for sexist language and adjectives that exclude or in any way demean girls or women. Look for use of the male pronoun to refer to both males and females. Although the generic use of the word *man* was accepted in the past, its use today is outmoded. The following examples show how sexist language can be avoided: *ancestors* instead of *forefathers; chairperson* instead of *chairman; community* instead of *brotherhood; firefighters* instead of *firemen; manufactured* instead of *manmade; the human family* instead of *the family of man*.

10. Look at the Copyright Date

Books on minority themes—usually hastily conceived—suddenly began appearing in the mid and late 1960s. There followed a growing number of "minority experience" books to meet the new market demand, but these books were still written by White authors, edited by White editors, and published by White publishers. They therefore reflected a White point of view. Not until the early 1970s did the children's book world begin to even remotely reflect the realities of a pluralistic society. The new direction resulted from the emergence of third-world authors writing about their own experiences in an oppressive society. This promising direction began reversing in the late 1970s. Nonsexist books, with rare exceptions, were not published before 1972 to 1974.

The copyright dates, therefore, can be a clue as to how likely the book is to be overtly racist or sexist, although a recent copyright date, of course, is no guarantee of a book's relevance or sensitivity. The copyright date only indicates the year in which the book was published. It usually takes two years—and often much more than that—from the time a manuscript is submitted to the publisher to the time it is actually printed and put on the market. This time lag meant very little in the past, but in a period of rapid change and new consciousness, when children's book publishing is attempting to be "relevant," it is becoming increasingly significant.

REFERENCES

Acuña, R. (1988). *Occupied America: A History of Chicanos.* (3rd ed.). New York: Harper & Row.

Allen, P. G. (1986). *The Sacred Hoop: Recovering the Feminine in American Indian Traditions.* Boston: Beacon Press.

Allport, G. W. (1954). *The Nature of Prejudice.* Reading, MA: Addison-Wesley.

Anderson, M. L., & Collins, P. H. (Eds.) (1992). *Race, Class, and Gender: An Anthology.* Belmont, CA: Wadsworth.

Apple, M. W., & Christian-Smith, L. K. (Eds.). (1991). *The Politics of the Textbook.* New York: Routledge.

Applebee, A. N. (1989). *A Study of Book-Length Works Taught in High School English Courses.* Albany, NY: Center for the Learning and Teaching of Literature.

Applebee, A. N. (1992). Stability and Change in the High-School Canon. *English Journal, 81,* 27–32.

Armitage, S. (1987). Through Women's Eyes: A New View of the West. In S. Armitage & E. Jameson (Eds.), *The Women's West* (pp. 9–18). Norman: University of Oklahoma Press.

Aronson, E., & Gonzalez, A. (1988). Desegregation, Jigsaw, and the Mexican-American Experience. In P. A. Katz & D. A. Taylor (Eds.), *Eliminating Racism: Profiles in Controversy* (pp. 301–314). New York: Plenum.

Asante, M. K. (1987). *The Afrocentric Idea.* Philadelphia: Temple University Press.

Banks, C. A. M. (1993). Parents and Teachers: Partners in Multicultural Education. In J. A. Banks & C. A. M. Banks (Eds.), *Multicultural Education: Issues and Perspectives* (2nd ed., pp. 332–351). Boston: Allyn and Bacon.

Banks, J. A. (Ed.). (1973). *Teaching Ethnic Studies: Concepts and Strategies.* 43rd Yearbook. Washington, DC: National Council for the Social Studies.

Banks, J. A. (1988a). Approaches to Multicultural Curriculum Reform. *Multicultural Leader, 1,* no. 2, 1–3.

Banks, J. A. (1988b). Ethnicity, Class, Cognitive and Motivational Styles: Research and Teaching Implications. *The Journal of Negro Education, 57,* 452–466.

Banks, J. A. (1991a) *Teaching Strategies for Ethnic Studies* (5th ed.). Boston: Allyn and Bacon.

Banks, J. A. (1991b). Multicultural Education: Its Effects on Students' Racial and Gender Role Attitudes. In J. P. Shaver (Ed.), *Handbook of Research on Social Studies Teaching and Learning* (pp. 459–469). New York: Macmillan.

Banks, J. A. (1993a). The Canon Debate, Knowledge Construction, and Multicultural Education. *Educational Researcher, 22* (5), 4–14.

Banks, J. A. (1993b). Multicultural Education for Young Children: Racial and Ethnic Attitudes and Their Modification. In B. Spodek (Ed.), *Handbook of Research on the Education of Young Children* (pp. 236–250). New York: Macmillan.

Banks, J. A. (1994). *Multiethnic Education Theory and Practice* (3rd ed.). Boston: Allyn and Bacon.

Banks, J. A., & Banks, C. A. M. (1983). The Self-Concept, Locus of Control, and Racial Attitudes of Preschool and Primary Grade Black Children Who Live in Predominantly White Suburban Communities. The University of Washington, Seattle, unpublished paper.

Banks, J. A., & Banks, C. A. M. (Eds.) (1993). *Multicultural Education: Issues and Perspectives* (2nd ed.). Boston: Allyn and Bacon.

Banks, J. A., Cortés, C. E., Gay, G., Garcia, R. L., & Ochoa, A. (1992). *Curriculum Guidelines for Multicultural Education* (rev. ed.). Washington, DC: National Council for the Social Studies.

Banks, J. A., & Lynch, J. (Eds.). (1986). *Multicultural Education in Western Societies.* London: Cassell.

Banks, J. A., with Clegg, A. A., Jr. (1990). *Teaching Strategies for the Social Studies* (4th ed.). White Plains, NY: Longman.

Banks, J. A., with Sebesta, S. L. (1982). *We Americans: Our History and People* (Vols. 1 and 2). Boston: Allyn and Bacon.

Bates, D. (1987). *The Long Shadow of Little Rock.* Fayetteville: University of Arkansas Press.

Becker, J. M. (Ed.). (1979). *Schooling for a Global Age.* New York: McGraw-Hill.

Bell, D. (1973). *The Coming of the Post-Industrial Society: A Venture in Social Forecasting.* New York: Basic Books.

Bernal, M. (1987). *The Afroasiatic Roots of Classical Civilization. Vol. 1: The Fabrication of Ancient Greece 1785–1985.* New Brunswick: Rutgers University Press.

Branch, T. (1988). *Parting the Waters: America in the King Years 1954–63.* New York: Simon and Schuster.

Brinton, C. (1962). *The Anatomy of Revolution.* New York: Vintage.

Brookover, W. B., & Erickson, E. L. (1969). *Society, Schools, and Learning.* Boston: Allyn and Bacon.

Brookover, W., et al. (1979). *School Social Systems and Student Achievement: Schools Can Make a Difference.* New York: Praeger.

Brophy, J., & Good, T. (1970). Teachers' Communication of Differential Expectations for Children's Classroom Performance: Some Behavioral Data. *Journal of Educational Psychology, 61,* 365–374.

Burns, G. M. (1978). *Leadership.* New York: Harper & Row.

Business-Higher Education Forum. (1990). *Three Realities: Minority Life in the United States.* Washington, DC: American Council on Education.

Butler, J. E., & Walter, J. C. (Eds.). (1991). *Transforming the Curriculum: Ethnic Studies and Women's Studies.* Albany: State University of New York Press.

Carter, D. J., & Wilson, R. (1991). *Minorities in Higher Education.* Ninth Annual Status Report. Washington, DC: American Council on Education.

Chmelynski, C. (1990). Controversy Attends Schools with All-Black, All-Male Classes. *The Executive Educator, 12,* 16–18.

Clark, K. B. (1963). *Prejudice and Your Child* (2nd ed., enlarged). Boston: Beacon Press.

Clark, K. B., & Clark, M. P. (1939). The Development of Consciousness of Self and the Emergence of Racial Identification in Negro Preschool Children. *Journal of Social Psychology, 10,* 591–599.

Clark, K. B., & Clark, M. P. (1950). Emotional Factors in Racial Identification and Preference in Negro Children. *Journal of Negro Education, 19,* 341–350.

Clarke, J. H. (1990). African People on My Mind. In A. G. Hilliard III, L. Payton-Stewart, & L. O. Williams (Eds.), *African American Content in the School Curriculum: Proceedings of the First National Conference* (pp. 51–59). Morristown, NJ: Aaron Press.

Code, L. (1991). *What Can She Know? Feminist Theory and the Construction of Knowledge.* Ithaca, NY: Cornell University Press.

Cohen, E. (1986). *Designing Groupwork: Strategies for Heterogeneous Classrooms.* New York: Teachers College Press.

Cole, M., John-Steiner, V., Scribner, S., & Souberman, E. (Eds.). (1978). *L. S. Vygotsky, Mind in Society: The Development of Higher Psychological Processes.* Cambridge, MA: Harvard University Press.

Coleman, J. S. et al. (1966). *Equality of Educational Opportunity.* Washington, DC: U.S. Government Printing Office.

Collins, P. H. (1990). *Black Feminist Thought: Knowledge, Consciousness, and the Politics of Empowerment.* New York: Routledge.

Comer, J. P. (1980). *School Power: Implications of an Intervention Project.* New York: Free Press.

Comer, J. P. (1988). Educating Poor Minority Children. *Scientific American, 259,* no. 5, 42–48.

Commission on Minority Participation in Education and American Life. (1988). *One-Third of a Nation.* Washington, DC: The American Council on Education.

Cortés, C. E. (1986). The Education of Language Minority Students: A Contextual Interaction Model. In California State Department of Education (Ed.), *Beyond Language: Social and Cultural Factors in Schooling Language Minority Students* (pp. 3–33). Los Angeles: California State University.

Crawford, J. (1989). *Bilingual Education: History, Politics, Theory and Practice.* Trenton, NJ: Crane.

Cremin, L. A. (1989). *Popular Education and Its Discontents.* New York: Harper & Row.

Cross, W. E., Jr. (1991). *Shades of Black: Diversity in African-American Identity.* Philadelphia: Temple University Press.

Cuban, L. (1989). The "At-Risk" Label and the Problem of Urban School Reform. *Phi Delta Kappan, 70,* 780–801.

D'Souza, D. (1991). *Illiberal Education: The Politics of Race and Sex on Campus.* New York: Free Press.

Daley, S. (1990). Inspirational History Draws Academic Fire. *The New Times,* October 10, pp. B8 ff.

Daniels, R. (1988). *Asian America: Chinese and Japanese in the United States Since 1850.* Seattle: University of Washington Press.

Davidson, N. (Ed.). (1984). *Cooperative Learning in Mathematics: A Handbook for Teachers.* Menlo Park, CA: Addison-Wesley.

Delpit, L. D. (1988). The Silenced Dialogue: Power and Pedagogy in Educating Other People's Children. *Harvard Educational Review, 58,* 280–298.

Drake, St. C. (1987). *Black Folk Here and There* (Vol. 1). Los Angeles: Center for Afro-American Studies, University of California.

DuBois, W. E. B. (1935). *Black Reconstruction.* Millwood, NY: Kraus-Thomson Organization Limited.

Edelman, M. R. (1992). *The Measure of Our Success: A Letter to My Children and Yours.* Boston: Beacon Press.

Edmonds, R. (1986). Characteristics of Effective Schools. In U. Neisser (Ed.), *The School Achievement of Minority Children: New Perspectives* (pp. 93–104). Hillsdale, NJ: Erlbaum.

Finn, C. E., Jr. (1990). Why Can't Colleges Convey Our Diverse Culture's Unifying Themes?" *The Chronicle of Higher Education, 36,* 40.

Ford Foundation, Project on Social Welfare and the American Future. (1989). *The Common Good: Social Welfare and the American Future.* New York: Ford Foundation.

Franklin, J. H., & Moss, A. A., Jr. (1988). *From Slavery to Freedom: A History of Negro Americans* (6th ed.). New York: Knopf.

Garcia, J. (in press). The Changing Image of Ethnic Groups in Textbooks. *Phi Delta Kappan.*

Garcia, R. L. (1993). Prepublication review of the manuscript for this book: *An Introduction to Multicultural Education.*

Gardner, H. (1983). *Frames of Mind: The Theory of Multiple Intelligences.* New York: Basic Books.

Gibbs, J. T. (Ed.). (1988). *Young, Black, and Male in America: An Endangered Species.* Dover, MA: Auburn House.

Golden, R., et al. (1991). *Dangerous Memories: Invasion and Resistance Since 1492.* Chicago: The Chicago Religious Task Force on Central America.

Goodman, M. E. (1952). *Race Awareness in Young Children.* New York: Collier Books.

Gordon, M. M. (1964). *Assimilation in American Life: The Role of Race, Religion and National Origins.* New York: Oxford University Press.

Gould, S. J. (1981). *The Mismeasure of Man.* New York: Norton.

Graff, G. (1992). *Beyond the Cultural Wars: How Teaching the Conflicts Can Revitalize American Education.* New York: Norton.

Graham, P. A. (1992). *S-O-S: Save Our Schools.* New York: Hill and Wang.

Grant, C. A., & Sleeter, C. E. (1986). *After the School Bell Rings.* London: Falmer Press.

Gray, P. (1991, July 8). "Whose America?" *Time, 138,* 13–17.

Greene, M. (1988). *The Dialectic of Freedom.* New York: Teachers College Press.

Hale-Benson, J. E. (1986). *Black Children: Their Roots, Cultures, and Learning styles* (rev. ed.). Baltimore: Johns Hopkins University Press.

Harding, S. (1991). *Whose Knowledge? Whose Science: Thinking from Women's Lives.* Ithaca, NY: Cornell University Press.

Heath, S. B. (1983). *Ways with Words: Language, Life and Work in Communities and Classrooms.* New York: Cambridge University Press.

Henry, W. A., III (1990, April 9). Beyond the Melting Pot. *Time,* 28–31.

Here They Come, Ready or Not. (1986, May 14). *Education Week.* Special issue.

Hirsch, E. D. (1987). *Cultural Literacy: What Every American Needs to Know.* Boston: Houghton Mifflin.

Hodgkinson, H. L. (1985). *All One System: Demographics in Education, Kindergarten through Graduate School.* Washington, DC: The Institute for Educational Leadership.

Hodgkinson, H. (1991). Reform Versus Reality. *Phi Delta Kappan, 73,* 9–16.

Howe, I. (1991, February 18). The Value of the Canon. *The New Republic, 204,* 40–44.

Hurston, Z. N. (1978). *Their Eyes Were Watching God.* Urbana: University of Illinois Press.

Irvine, J. J. (1990). *Black Students and School Failure: Policies, Practices, and Prescriptions.* New York: Praeger.

Jane, L. C. (1989). *The Journal of Christopher Columbus.* New York: Bonanza Books.

Johnson, W. B., & Packer, A. B. (1987) *Workforce 2000: Work and Workers for the 21st Century.* Washington, DC: U.S. Government Printing Office.

Jones, J. (1985). *Labor of Love, Labor of Sorrow: Black Women, Work, and the Family from Slavery to the Present.* New York: Basic Books.

Katz, P. A. (1973). Perception of Racial Cues in Preschool Children: A New Look. *Developmental Psychology, 8,* 295–299.

Katz, P. A., & Zalk, S. R. (1978). Modification of Children's Racial Attitudes. *Developmental Psychology, 14,* 447–461.

Keen, B. (Trans.). (1959). *The Life of the Admiral Christopher Columbus By His Son Ferdinand.* New Brunswick, NJ: Rutgers University Press.

King, M. L. (1987). Selected by C. S. King. *The Words of Martin Luther King, Jr.* New York: Newmarket Press.

Klausmeier, H. J., & Goodwin, W. (1971). *Learning and Human Abilities: Educational Psychology* (4th ed.) New York: Harper & Row.

Kochman, T. (1981). *Black and White Styles in Conflict.* Chicago: University of Chicago Press.

Kuhn, T. S. (1970). *The Structure of Scientific Revolutions* (2nd ed., enlarged). Chicago: University of Chicago Press.

Lasker, B. (1929). *Race Attitudes in Children.* New York: Holt.

Ladson-Billings, G. (1990) Like Lightning in a Bottle: Attempting to Capture the Pedagogical Excellence of Successful Teachers of Black Students. *International Journal of Qualitative Studies in Education, 3,* 335–344.

Lee, C. D. (1992). Profile of an Independent Black Institution: African-Centered Education at Work. *The Journal of Negro Education, 61,* 160–177.

Leo, J. (1989). Teaching History the Way It Happened. *U.S. News and World Report, 202,* 73.

Lightfoot, S. L. (1988). *Balm in Gilead: Journey of a Healer,* Reading, MA: Addison-Wesley.

Litcher, J. H., & Johnson, D. W. (1969). Changes in Attitudes toward Negroes of White Elementary School Students After Use of Multiethnic Readers. *Journal of Educational Psychology, 60,* 148–152.

Litcher, J. H., Johnson, D. W., & Ryan, F. L. (1973). Use of Pictures of Multiethnic Interaction to Change Attitudes of White Elementary School Students Toward Blacks. *Psychological Reports, 33,* 367–372.

Lynch, J. (1986). *Multicultural Education: Principles and Practice.* London: Routledge and Kegan Paul.

McConnell, S., & Breindel, E. (1990, January 8 and 15). Head to Come. *The New Republic,* pp. 19–21.

Mercer, J. R. (1989). Alternative Paradigms for Assessment in a Pluralistic Society. In J. A. Banks & C. A. M. Banks (Eds.), *Multicultural Education: Issues and Perspectives* (pp. 289–304). Boston: Allyn and Bacon.

Minami, M., & Kennedy, B. P. (Eds.). (1992). *Language Issues in Literacy and Bilingual/Multicultural Educaiton.* Cambridge, MA: Harvard Educational Review Reprint Series #22.

Modgil, S., Verma, G. K., Mallick, K., & Modgil, C. (Eds.). (1986). *Multicultural Education: The Interminable Debate.* London: Falmer Press.

Morison, S. E. (1974). *The European Discovery of America, The Southern Voyages 1492–1616.* New York: Oxford University Press.

Muir, K. (1990). Eyes on the Prize: A Review. Paper submitted to J. A. Banks as partial requirement for the course EDUC 423, Educating Diverse Groups. Seattle: University of Washington.

Muzzey, D. S. (1915). *Readings in American History.* Boston: Ginn.

Myrdal, G. (with Sterner, R., & Rose, A.). (1944). *An American Dilemma: The Negro Problem and Modern Democracy.* New York: Harper & Row.

National Council for the Accreditation of Teacher Education. (1977). *Standards for the Accreditation of Teacher Education.* Washington, DC: Author.

Neihardt, J. G. (1972). *Black Elk Speaks: Being the Life Story of a Holy Man of the Oglala Sioux.* New York: Pocket Books.

New York (City) Board of Education. (1989). *Statement of Policy on Multicultural Education and Promotion of Positive Intergroup Relations.* New York: Author.

Oakes, J. (1992). Can Tracking Research Inform Practice? Technical, Normative, and Political Considerations. *Educational Researcher, 21,* (4) 12–21.

Olsen, F. (1974). *On the Trail of the Arawaks.* Norman: University of Oklahoma Press.

Orwell, G. (1946). *Animal Farm.* New York: Harcourt Brace.

Ovando, C. J., & Collier, V. P. (1985). *Bilingual and ESL Classrooms: Teaching in Multicultural Contexts.* New York: McGraw-Hill.

Pallas, A. M., Natriello, G., & McDill, E. L. (1989). The Changing Nature of the Disadvantaged Population: Current Dimensions and Future Trends. *Educational Researcher, 18,* (5), 16–22.

Parekh, B. (1986). The Concept of Multicultural Education. In S. Modgil, G. K. Verma, K. Mallick, & C. Modgil (Eds.), *Multicultural Education: The Interminable Debate* (pp. 19–31). Philadelphia: Falmer Press.

Parker, W. P. (1991). *Multicultural Education in Democratic Societies.* Paper presented at the annual meeting of the American Educational Research Association, Chicago.

Parks, R., with Haskins, J. (1992). *Rosa Parks: My Story.* New York: Dial.

Patton, J. M. (1992). Assessment and Identification of African-American Learners with Gifts and Talents. *Exceptional Children, 59,* 150–159.

Percell, C. H. (1993). Social Class and Educational Equality. In J. A. Banks & C. A. M. Banks (Eds.), *Multicultural Education: Issues and Perspectives* (2nd ed., pp. 71–89). Boston: Allyn and Bacon.

Peters, W. (1987). *A Class Divided: Then and Now* (expanded edition). New Haven, CT: Yale University Press.

Philips, S. U. (1983). *The Invisible Culture: Communication in a Classroom and Community on the Warm Spring Indian Reservation.* New York: Longman.

Ponce de Leon, J. (1992). The Native American Response to the Columbus Quincentenary. *Multicultural Review, 1,* 20–22.

Quality Education for Minorities Project. (1990). *Education that Works: An Action Plan for the Education of Minorities.* Cambridge, MA: Massachusetts Institute of Technology.

Ramírez, M., III, & Castañeda, A. (1974). *Cultural Democracy, Bicognitive Development and Education.* New York: Academic Press.

Ravitch, D. (1990a). Diversity and Democracy: Multicultural Education in America. *American Educator, 14,* 16–20 ff. 46–48.

Ravitch, D. (1990b). Multiculturalism Yes, Particularism No. *The Chronicle of Higher Education,* A44.

Reschly, D. J. (1988). Minority MMR Overrepresentation and Special Education Reform. *Exceptional Children, 54,* 316–323.

Richardson, V., Casanova, U., Placier, P., & Guilfoyle, K. (1989). *School Children at Risk.* London: Falmer Press.

Richman, L. S. (1990, April 9). The Coming World Labor Shortage. *Fortune,* 70–77.

Rodriguez, C. E. (1989). *Puerto Ricans Born in the U.S.A.* Boston: Unwin Hyman.

Rosenthal, R., & Jacobson, L. (1968). *Pygmalion in the Classroom: Teacher Expectations and Pupils' Intellectual Development.* New York: Holt, Rinehart & Winson.

Rouse, I. (1992). *The Tainos: Rise and Decline of the People Who Greeted Columbus.* New Haven, CT: Yale University Press.

Samuda, R. J. (1975). *Psychological Testing of American Minorities: Issues and Consequences.* New York: Dodd, Mead.

Schlesinger, A. (1991). *The Disuniting of America: Reflections on a Multicultural Society.* Knoxville: Whittle Direct Books.

Shade, B. J. (1982). Afro-American Cognitive Style. *Review of Educational Research, 52,* 210–244.

Shade, B. R. (Ed.). (1989). *Culture, Style, and the Educative Process.* Springfield, IL: Charles C. Thomas.

Shirts, G. (1969). *Starpower.* LaJolla, CA: Western Behavioral Science Institute.

Sirkin, G. (1990, January 18). The Multiculturalists Strike Again. *The Wall Street Journal,* p. A14.

Slavin, R. E. (1983). *Cooperative Learning.* New York: Longman.

Sleeter, C. E., & Grant, C. A. (1987). An Analysis of Multicultural Education in the United States. *Harvard Educational Review, 57,* 421–444.

Sleeter, C. E., & Grant, C. A. (1988). *Making Choices for Multicultural Education: Five Approaches to Race, Class and Gender.* Columbus, OH: Merrill.

Smitherman, G. (1977). *Talkin and Testifyin: The Language of Black America.* Boston: Houghton Mifflin.

Snipp, C. M. (1989). *American Indians: The First of this Land.* New York: Russel Sage Foundation.

Spencer, M. B. (1982). Personal and Group Identity of Black Children: An Alternative Synthesis. *Genetic Psychology Monographs, 106,* 59–84.

Spencer, M. B. (1984). Black Children's Race Awareness, Racial Attitudes, and Self-Concept: A Reinterpretation. *Journal of Child Psychology and Psychiatry, 25,* 433–441.

Staff of *Fortune.* (1990, March 26). An American Vision for the 1990s. *Fortune,* pp. 14, 16.

Stahl, R. J., & VanSickle, R. L. (Eds.). (1992). *Cooperative Learning in the Social Studies Classroom.* Bulletin No. 87. Washington, DC: National Council for the Social Studies.

Stannard, D. E. (1992). *American Holocaust: Columbus and the Conquest of the New World.* New York: Oxford University Press.

Stephan, W. G. (1985). Intergroup Relations. In G. Lindzey & E. Aronson (Eds.), *The Handbook of Social Psychology* (Vol. 2, 3rd ed., pp. 599–658). Hillsdale, NJ: Erlbaum.

Sue, D. W. (Ed.). (1981). *Counseling the Culturally Different: Theory and Practice.* New York: Wiley.

Taba, H., et al. (1971). *A Teacher's Handbook to Elementary Social Studies: An Inductive Approach.* Reading, MA: Addison-Wesley.

Takaki, R. (1989). *Strangers from a Different Shore: A History of Asian Americans.* Boston: Little, Brown.

Theodorson, G. A., & Theodorson, A. G. (1969). *A Modern Dictionary of Sociology.* New York: Barnes & Noble.

Toffler, A. (1980) *The Third Wave.* New York: William Morrow.

Tomasi, L. F. (Ed.). (1985). *Italian Americans: New Perspectives in Italian Immigration and Ethnicity.* New York: Center for Migration Studies of New York.

Trager, H. G., & Yarrow, M. R. (1952). *They Learn What They Live: Prejudice in Young Children.* New York: Harper and Brothers.

U.S. Bureau of the Census. (1992). *Statistical Abstract of the United States* (112th ed.). Washington, DC: U.S. Government Printing Office.

U.S. Companies Are in a Global War for Survival. (1989, May 28). *The New York Times.*

van den Berghe, P. (1978). *Race and Racism: A Comparative Perspective.* 2nd ed. New York: Wiley.

Van Sertima, I. V. (Ed.). (1984). *Black Women in Antiquity.* New Brunswick, NJ: Transaction Books.

Verma, G. K. (Ed.). (1989). *Education for All: A Landmark in Pluralism.* London: Falmer Press.

Vogt, L. A., Jordan, C., & Tharp, R. G. (1987). Explaining School Failure, Producing School Success: Two Cases. *Anthropology & Education Quarterly, 18,* 277–286.

Weatherford, J. (1992). *Native Roots: How the Indians Enriched America.* New York: Fawcett Columbine.

Wertsch, J. V. (1985). *Vygotsky and the Social Formation of the Mind.* Cambridge, MA: Harvard University Press.

White, J. L., & Parham, T. A. (1990). *The Psychology of Blacks: An African-American Perspective* (2nd ed.) Englewood Cliffs, NJ: Prentice Hall.

Williams, F. (Ed.). (1970). *Language and Poverty: Perspectives on a Theme.* Chicago: Markham.

Williams, J. E., & Edwards, C. D. (1969). An Exploratory Study of the Modification of Color and Racial Concept Attitudes in Preschool Children. *Child Development, 40,* 737–750.

Williams, J. E., & Morland, J. K. (1976). *Race, Color and the Young Child.* Chapel Hill: University of North Carolina Press.

Wilson, W. J. (1987). *The Truly Disadvantaged: The Inner City, the Underclass, and Public Policy.* Chicago: University of Chicago Press.

Woodson, C. G. (1921). *The History of the Negro Church.* Washington, DC: The Associated Publishers.

Zigmond, N. (Ed.). (1992). Issues in the Education of African-American Youth in Special Education Settings. Special Issue. *Exceptional Children, 59,* 99–176.

INDEX

Acculturation, defined, 56
Achievement
    academic, increasing, 38
    approaches to multicultural education, 8, 9 (table)
Additive approach to multicultural education, 8, 25–26
African Americans
    characteristics of, 53
    college enrollment, 33
    economic status, 55
    educational attainment, 33
    instructional strategies, effective, 44
    population, 34, 55
    self-determination, 54
    sense of peoplehood, 54
    social-class schism within, 35–36
    unemployment, teens, 33
Afrocentric
    curriculum, 4
    defined, 21–22
Allport, Gordon W., 44, 45
American dilemma, 52
American Indians. See Native Americans
Applebee, Arthur N., 3, 19
Asante, Molefi K., 21–22
Asian Americans
    economic status, 55
    population, 34, 40, 55

Assessment, 12, 17
Assimilation, defined, 56
At-risk, 8
Attitudes. See also Intergroup education; Prejudice
    modifying, 42–44
    racial, children's, 40–44
    relationship to achievement, 10, 17

Banks, Cherry A. McGee, 38
Banks, James A., 28, 81–90
Banks' Value Inquiry Model, 77
Baratz, Joan, 49–50
Bell, Daniel, 32
Bernal, Martin, 5
Bilingual education, Hispanic perspective on, 54
Biography, use in multicultural education, 88
Black English, 11, 49, 53–54
Brinton, Crane, 75
Burns, James M., 37

Canon, debate over, 2–3, 22–24
Civil rights, organizations, 54
Civil Rights Movement, 5–6
Clark, Kenneth B., 41
Clark, Mamie, 41
Columbus and the Arawaks, 65–71
Columbus, Christopher, 65–71, 95
Comer, James P. , 38

Concepts
  defined, 59–60
  defining, 74–75
  identifying, 61–62
  key, 52, 53 (table), 54–58, 61
  spiraling, 62–63
  use in teaching, 60, 79
Cooperative learning, 43–44, 50
Counseling students, 12
Cross, William E., Jr., 41
Cultural deprivation
  defined, 8
  compared to cultural difference, 8
  paradigm, characteristics of, 48–49
Cultural difference
  defined, 8
  compared to cultural deprivation, 8
  paradigm, characteristics of, 49–50
Culture
  definitions of, 50–51
  macroculture, defined, 51
  microcultures, 51–52
  school, 12
Curriculum
  conceptual, 61–62
  Eurocentric, 10, 11 (table), 19–20,
    83–84, 95
  hidden, 12
  infusion, defined, 15
  mainstream, challenges to, 19–21
  multicultural, 10, 11 (table), 82–
    83, 95–96
  reform approaches, 8, 9 (table),
    24, 25 (figure), 95–96
  spiral, 62–64
  transformation, 15, 79
*Curriculum Guidelines for Multicultural
  Education*, 93

Data
  collecting, 75
  evaluating, 75–77
Decision-making and social action
    approach to multicultural educa-
    tion, 8, 25 (figure), 27
Demographic

imperative, defined, 4, 31–35
  trends, 31–35
Discovery, problematizing, 65–71,
  83–84, 95
Discrimination. *See also* Attitudes; In-
    tergroup education; Prejudice; Ra-
    cism
  concept, key, 55, 61
  lesson on, 78–79
Disproportionality, 97

Edmonds, Ronald R., 38
Education for freedom, defined, 81–82
Elliott, Jane, 28
Encapsulation, cultural, 1, 7
Ethnic diversity
  generalizations about, 63 (table)
  key concept, 61
  teaching about, 63 (table)
Ethnic studies
  knowledge base, 52
  universities implementing require-
    ments, 20
European Americans
  diversity within, 20, 88
  economic status, 55
  encounter with Native Americans,
    82–84
  labor force, in, 34
  population, 34, 40, 55

Figures
  A Model of Social Inquiry, 72
  Approaches to Multicultural Cur-
    riculum Reform, 25
  Conceptual Approach to Teaching
    Social Protest, 64
  Multicultural Benchmarks, 92
Filipino Americans, social status of,
  54–55

Gardner, Howard, 94
Generalizations
  defined, 59–60
  identifying, 62
  spiraling, 62–63

Global education
  compared to multicultural education, 18
  defined, 17
Graff, Gerald, 3
Grant, Carl A., 16
Greene, Maxine, 1

Hirsch, E.D., 24
Hispanics
  bilingual education, view of, 54
  economic status, 55
  educational attainment, 33
  Mexican Americans, origins of, 53
  population, 34–35, 40
  sense of peoplehood, 54
  social-class schism within, 35–36
Historical bias, teaching about, 65–71
Hodgkinson, Harold L., 32, 94

Identity
  ethnic, 54
  group, defined, 41
  personal, defined, 41
  racial, 41–42
  reference, defined, 41
Immigration
  Asia, from, 34
  Europe, from, 34
  Latin America, from, 34
  U.S. population, origins of, 53
Instructional materials, 12
Intergroup education. *See also* Attitudes; Prejudice; Racism
  approaches to multicultural education, 8, 9 (table), 10
Interview with James A. Banks, 81–90
Intraethnic diversity, key concept, 55–56
Italian Americans, 53

Japanese Americans, self-determination, 54
Jewish Americans
  self-determination, 54
  sense of peoplehood, 54

Johnson, David W., 44
Katz, Phyllis A., 43, 44, 84–85
King, Martin Luther, Jr., 17
Knowledge
  construction process, 57–58, 65–71
  categories of, 60
  components necessary for effective teaching, 47, 52
  as a social construction, 5

Languages, response of the school to, 11–12
Latinos. *See* Hispanics
Labov, William, 49
Leadership
  transactional, defined, 37
  transformational, defined, 37
Learning styles, 11
Lessons, sample. *See also* Teaching strategies
  Columbus and the Arawaks (example of knowledge construction), 65–71
  Trying to Buy a Home in Lakewood Island, 78–79
  unit on revolutions, 71–77
  value inquiry, 77–79
Lightfoot, Sara Lawrence, 27–28
Litcher, John H., 43, 44
Lockwood, Ann Turnbaugh, 81

Madison Center, 22
Materials, instructional, 11, 19, 88–89, 96–97
Mexican Americans. *See* Hispanics
Monitoring, developing a plan, 98–99
Morland, John K., 42
Multicultural education
  approaches, 8–10, 24–27
  assumptions of, 16–17
  benchmarks, 92 (figure)
  challenges to, 21–22
  confusion about, 16–18, 89–90
  contexts of, 87–89
  debate over, 2–3
  defined, 1, 81

democratic ideal, 5–6
European Americans, including,
    17–19
evidence supporting, 84–86
goals of, 1–2, 6, 16–18, 37, 40, 64,
    81, 97
materials for, 88–89
paradigm, 48–49
policy statement, 91–93
self, exploration of, 88
skill, developing, 64–65
staff, school, 93–95
Western civilization, reinterpreta-
    tion of, 4–6
Multicultural literacy, 24
Multicultural schools, characteristics
    of, 10–12
Myrdal, Gunnar, 52

National Association of Multicultural
    Education, 22
National Association of Scholars, 22
National Council for the Accredita-
    tion of Teacher Education, 96
National Council for the Social Stud-
    ies, 93
Native Americans
    European encounter with, 82–84,
        95–96
    lesson on, 65–71
    origins of, 53
    school experience of, 37
New York (City) Board of Education,
    92–93

Oakes, Jeannie, 38
Olsen, Fred, 69, 83
Orwell, George, 77

Parent involvement, 97
Perspectives
    key concept, 54
    multiple, 82–84
Policies, multicultural, 91–93
Population
    African American, 34

aging of, 33, 40
    Asian American, 34, 40
    Hispanic American, 34–35, 40
    immigration, influence on, 34–35
    people of color, 35
    statistics on, 4, 21, 32
    White, 34
    workforce needs, 33–35
Post-industrial society, defined, 32
Power, 3
Powerful ideas. *See* Concepts, key
Prejudice. *See also* Attitudes; Inter-
    group education; Racism
    defined, 55
    key concept, 61
    reduction, 40, 42–45, 84–85
    White bias, 85
Primary resources, using in a lesson,
    65–71
Public interest, 23

Questions
    examples, 71, 76 (table), 79, 89
    formulating, 73

Racism. *See also* Attitudes; Intergroup
    education; Prejudice
    institutional, 55
    key concept, 55
Restructuring, school. *See also* School
    reform
    defined, 37
    goals of, 39
    policy statement, importance of,
        91–93
Revolution
    American Revolution, 71, 75, 76
        (table), 77
    defined, 56, 75
    key concept, 56–57
    Mexican Revolution, 71, 75, 76 (ta-
        ble), 77
    Pueblo Revolution, 71, 75, 76 (ta-
        ble), 77
    teaching about, 71–77
Richman, L., 33

School reform, 10–13, 17, 36–37, 95–97. *See also* Restructuring, school
Sense of peoplehood, 54
Slavin, Robert E., 50
Sleeter, Christine E., 16
Social action, 8, 27, 39
Social class
  children in poverty, 36, 40
  divisions, 6, 35
Social protest
  example, 60 (table)
  generalizations, 60 (table)
  spiraling, 63, 64 (table)
Social science inquiry
  model, 72 (figure)
  unit on revolutions, 71–77
Societal reform, need for, 39
Special interest, defined, 23
Spencer, Margaret B., 41
Staff, school
  attitudes, 94–95
  diversity of, importance, 93
  policies for diversification of, 94
Star Power, simulation game, 73

Taba, Hilda, 61, 62
Tables
  Approaches to Multicultural Education, 9
  Categories of Knowledge, 60
  Eight Characteristics of the Multicultural School, 11
  Key Concepts to Guide the Study of Ethnic and Cultural Groups, 53
  Teaching Ethnic Diversity in all Subject Areas, 63
Teachers
  changes necessary for multicultural education, 86
  education programs for, 96
  empowering, 38–39
  expectations, 94–95

knowledge, needed for multicultural teaching, 47, 52
  paradigm shifts, 86–87
Teachers for a Democratic Society, 22
Teaching strategies. *See also* Lessons, sample
  formulating, 62
  multicultural, 96
Testing, 12. *See also* Assessment
Textbooks, 11, 19, 88–89, 96–97
Toffler, Alvin, 32
Tracking, 38
Trager, Helen G., 43
Transformation
  approach to multicultural education, 8, 25 (figure), 26–27
  curriculum, 15, 27
Trying to Buy a Home in Lakewood Island, 78–79

Underclass, defined, 35

Value inquiry
  Banks' model, 77
  example, 77–79
  skills, developing, 64–65
  Trying to Buy a Home in Lakewood Island, 78–79
Values, American Creed, 52
Voices, multiple, 82–83

Western civilization, reinterpreting, 4–5
Western traditionalists, defined, 2
Wilson, William J., 6
Workforce, changing nature of, 31–35

Vygotsky, Lev Semyonovich, 57

Yarrow, Marian R., 43

Zalk, Susan R., 43, 44, 84–85